KEYS TO PARENTING THE ONLY CHILD

Carl E. Pickhardt, Ph.D.

BARRON'S

Cover photo © 1997 PhotoDisc, Inc.

The material in this book is drawn from my experience counseling with many only children and their parents, as well as from conducting numerous parenting workshops over the years. All examples and quotes given, however, are fictional inventions created to illustrate a psychological point.

Acknowledgments

I would like to thank my wife, Irene, for her editorial help during the final stages of this manuscript, and the Barbara Bauer Literary Agency for continuing to find the *right* publishers for my books.

All inquiries should be addressed to:
Barron's Educational Series, Inc.
250 Wireless Boulevard
Hauppauge, New York 11788

Library of Congress Catalog Card No. 97-18747

International Standard Book No. 0-8120-9769-6

Library of Congress Cataloging-in-Publication Data
Pickhardt, Carl E.
    Keys to parenting the only child / Carl E. Pickhardt.
        p.   cm. — (Barron's parenting keys)
    Includes bibliographical references and index.
    ISBN 0-8120-9769-6
    1. Only child. 2. Only child—Psychology. 3. Parent and child.
    4. Parenting. I. Title. II. Series.
    HQ777.3.P53   1997
    306.874—dc21   97-18747
                                            CIP

PRINTED IN THE UNITED STATES OF AMERICA
987654321

CONTENTS

INTRODUCTION

Since the baby boom of the 1950s, families in this country have been growing smaller. Today, somewhere between 20 and 30 percent of dual- and single-parent families are limited to an only child. Many factors lie behind this change.

- There is more access to birth control and emphasis on family planning.
- There is more concern about overpopulation.
- There is the growing cost of financially supporting a large family.
- There are infertile couples for whom the expense of adoption precludes having more than one child.
- There are parents wanting to avoid the competing sibling demands and family complexity created by having multiple children.
- There are parents who want to satisfy their desires for career and parenthood by limiting family size at home.
- There are people marrying or remarrying at an older age, waiting longer to begin a family, and having fewer children in consequence.
- There are divorces occurring earlier in marriage, before larger families have had a chance to grow.
- And there are simply a lot of couples who are deciding that having a single child creates family enough.

In all these cases, parental choice tends to increase the incidence of only child families.

This book is for prospective parents who are weighing the pros and cons of an only child family, and for actual parents with a single child who, by voluntary choice or involuntary circumstance, are not going to add more to the one they already have. For either group, this book is intended to help these adults understand some of the problems and possibilities that go with parenting an only child. Most important, it is to help parents of only children dispel two myths.

- **Myth number one:** *Having an only child is less demanding than having multiple children.* In reality, parenting an only child is extremely demanding because this is the first and last child in one, the only chance for parenting that a mother and father get. They tend to take this responsibility extremely seriously: "We want to give our best and do it right, and we don't want to make any harmful mistakes." *Having an only child can be high-pressure parenting.*
- **Myth number two:** *Having an only child is less complicated than having multiple children.* It is true that competing demands and conflicts over sharing between two or more children are eliminated in the only child family. It is also true that the number of children to support and supervise has been reduced to a minimum. This circumstantial simplicity, however, can often create an increased degree of psychological complexity. Because parents find themselves extremely preoccupied with an only child, the sense of attachment can become very strong, responsible decision making can become very labor intensive, separation can be very painful, letting go can become hard to do, and an extremely emotionally sensitized relationship can develop between parents and child. "I never thought parenting a single child would be so difficult to figure out." *Having an only child can be interpersonally complex.*

Having an only child, like having multiple children, is double-edged. Only child families have certain strengths, but also certain risks.

Some of the *strengths* can include:

- being able to devote to the child undivided attention and all available parental resources;
- being able to experience a high degree of intimacy with this son or daughter;
- and being fully able to enjoy him or her undistracted by other children.

Some of the *risks* can include:

- extreme attention creating an exaggerated sense of self-importance and undue entitlement in the child;
- extreme attachment creating emotional dependence on parents;
- and close association with parents getting in the way of the child forming significant friendships with peers.

Common challenges that must usually be resolved for the only child and thus for the parents include:

- establishing an adequate sense of personal definition distinct from parents;
- achieving adequate emotional separation from parents;
- setting adequate boundaries of responsibility with parents;
- learning to live on terms of reciprocity with parents;
- and creating adequate social independence between the only child and parents.

This book describes many of the problems and possibilities commonly associated with parenting an only child. The conduct of parenting, like the conduct of all relationships, is a matter of choice. Hopefully, in reading about some of the complexities of raising an only child, parents will be encouraged to make choices that enhance the positive possibilities with their only child, and cause them to become more mindful of potential difficulties.

Because so many variables affect family functioning and an individual child's growth, simply being an only child does not guarantee a predictable set of characteristics that will develop or outcomes that will occur. The issues that are described in this book must be qualified: most of them apply to many only child families, but none of them apply to all. Only child families are too varied to fit a single stereotype. There are no absolutes that rule these families, only recurrent themes that commonly arise. *This book describes tendencies, not certainties.*

In addition, like any other children, only children can embody contradictions. In some ways they can be shy, in others outgoing. They can be both secure and insecure, self-centered and considerate of others, dependent and independent. Because first children are only children until the next sibling arrives, some of the issues described in this book will have relevance to parenting the first child as well.

In my counseling practice and in conducting parenting workshops, I have seen a disproportionate number of only children and their parents over the years. This overrepresentation is not because only child families have more problems than their multiple-child counterparts. Focused on one child and undistracted by others, parents of an only child have a heightened sensitivity to his or her well-being. Continually vigilant and naturally protective, they are quick to take preventive action, checking out concerns by seeking help rather than letting problems go and grow.

My overall impression has been, and continues to be, that only children tend to be extremely well-parented. These mothers and fathers take their family responsibilities seriously, they stay informed about what is going on in their child's life, and they rigorously supervise that child's conduct.

Organization of This Book

The sections of this book are organized as follows. Part One describes two powerful sources of influence built into the only child family system—the child's natural striving for similarity to parents, and his or her growing up in the absence of siblings. Part Two considers different family compositions that can have an impact on the only child, depending on whether he or she lives with a single parent or with two parents in the home. Part Three explores a series of issues having to do with being the center of family focus— attention, the "only" attitude, and self-image. Part Four examines the dynamic of closeness between the only child and parents in terms of attachment and in terms of intimacy. Part Five addresses three significant sources of pressure on the only child—seeking parental approval, meeting parental expectations, and satisfying parental ambition. Part Six deals with two issues of accountability—responsibility and obligation. Part Seven discusses two issues that do much to shape the only child's identity—individuality and a tendency toward extremes. Part Eight, the longest section, prepares parents for changes likely to occur in their only child during the teenage years, taking them through adolescence stage by stage—early adolescence, mid-adolescence, late adolescence, and trial independence. Part Nine gives attention to softening the effects of divorce, because when this event occurs, it is often particularly difficult for an only child. In the Questions and Answers section, a number of common parental concerns are addressed. Also included are a Glossary of terms that the reader may find unfamiliar and Suggested Reading that the reader may find helpful.

This book addresses either a set of issues that tend to characterize the only child's development or a dynamic that tends to be particularly relevant to only child family life. For each issue, two aspects are presented:

1. inherent *strengths* in that tendency are described and *strategies* for nurturing those strengths are suggested;
2. common *risks* in that tendency are identified and *strategies* for reducing those risks are recommended.

Throughout this book, it is important to remember that having an only child is *not* better or worse than having multiple children. Living with a single child brings one set of benefits and problems; living with several children brings another set of benefits and problems. Neither family is necessarily more healthy or happy than the other, nor is the parenting necessarily more easy or difficult with one child or several. Choosing to have one child simply accentuates a particular set of family dynamics and encourages certain developmental tendencies that can be somewhat more pronounced than in families where multiple children are present.

1

▲▲▲

FITTING IN

STRIVING FOR SIMILARITY TO PARENTS

The personality traits, values, and conduct of parents have enormous shaping effect on the development of their children, particularly during the impressionable years of early childhood. Beyond genetic similarity, there are three powerful interpersonal forces that encourage children to resemble their parents.

1. *Young children unconsciously copy their parents.* How these adults live within themselves (in a state of self-acceptance or self-rejection, for example), how these adults live with others (acting tolerant or critical, for example), and how these adults approach the world (with trust or suspicion, for example) all influence children unawares. Unknowingly, children tend to adopt similar beliefs, behaviors, and attitudes of their own. Growing up with parents for whom minor choices create an agony of worry, for example, may cause the child to experience anxiety when making decisions of his or her own. *Young children are powerfully affected simply by who and how their parents are.*

2. *Young children consciously copy their parents.* Admiration causes children to imitate their mother or father. For example, a little child may parrot the adult's opinions, thereby creating a satisfying sense

of commonality: "We think the same way!" The child may ask to help a parent make or fix something, thereby creating a rewarding sense of equality: "I can do what you do, too!" The child may ask to borrow parental belongings, thereby creating a sense of identification: "I can use what you use!" *Young children want to be like their parents.*

3. *Young children mostly agree to live on terms set by how their parents live.* Family systems are value systems that reflect the founding beliefs of the adults in charge. Parental authority is responsible for creating a set of regulations, limits, and demands within which children can securely and responsibly grow. *Obedience is an act of similarity.* Behaving how parents prescribe is usually rewarded with approval. Children feel closely connected to parents and in a state of favor when they conform to family expectations, comply with family rules, and cooperate with family requests. *Young children want to please their parents.*

Whereas these factors encourage similarity of children to parents in most families, *the force of these factors is greatly amplified when there is only one child,* and this includes the first child until a second arrives. In the only child family, the boy or girl often feels less freedom to be different from parents than in a multiple-child family because

- there are no siblings to exhibit contrasting traits and expand parental tolerance for individual variation;
- there are no siblings to develop a contrasting relationship with parents, and thus create more alternatives for parent/child interaction;
- and there are no siblings with whom to identify, only the parents.

The only child is born and raised in an adult family world: "I never told my parents, but the reason I wanted a brother or sister was to take some of their pressure off me. Because they treated me like one of them, I always felt I was supposed to be like them. If there had been other kids in the family, I think my parents would have treated me less as another adult and more like a child, and I would have felt more free to treat myself the same way."

It is easy for parents to "adultize" their only son or daughter, to encourage the boy or girl to act grown-up when he or she is actually still a child. Rewarded with approval for precociously acquiring some of the parents' older characteristics (like mature speech and social poise), the child appears to function in many situations on adult terms. This appearance, however, can mask a deficiency. Precious freedom to be a child and act immature may have been given up. "I never remember it being okay to be a child. I was always supposed to act my parents' age." In addition, parents may presume too much on the child's precocity by inappropriately sharing adult information (marital, financial, sexual) that he or she lacks the life experience to maturely evaluate and understand.

2

$\blacktriangleright\hspace{-2pt}\wedge\hspace{-2pt}\wedge\hspace{-2pt}\wedge\hspace{-2pt}\wedge\hspace{-2pt}\wedge\hspace{-2pt}\wedge\hspace{-2pt}\wedge\hspace{-2pt}\wedge\hspace{-2pt}\wedge\hspace{-2pt}\wedge\hspace{-2pt}\wedge\hspace{-2pt}\blacktriangleleft$

STRENGTHS FROM SIMILARITY

A STRONG SENSE OF FAMILY TRADITION

Extreme force of similarity to parents tends to rule the only child's family life, and in many ways this can assert a positive influence. Only children can be very clear about their convictions; they can be sure of themselves and can feel very well connected to their parents.

"I was never in any doubt about who I was, what was right, what kind of person I wanted to be. Even today, my values about right and wrong, even my tastes, are pretty much what my parents taught me to believe. They treated me so well and cared for me so much, I wanted to do my best to become like them. That's why we're such good friends now that I'm an adult. We had so much in common when I was growing up, and we still do. I had lots of teenage friends who fought to be different from their parents. Not me."

For many parents of only children, there is a very satisfying sense of successfully transmitting what they stand for to their only child who fulfills so many of their expectations. This similarity can create a *synergy of pleasing:*

- the more the only child exhibits similarity to parents,
- the more pleased parents are,
- the more pleasure they express,

4

- the more pleased the child is with himself or herself,
- the more the child wants to keep on pleasing them,
- the more pleased parents become by the similarity they see.

For many only children, there is a very deep and affirming sense of family heritage that connects them with parents: "I am proud to carry on the values and traditions of my parents." It is the desire to honor this heritage that causes such children to be very conservative about straying from the philosophy and style of life they have been taught. Risk takers in other ways, they are usually not risk takers in this—significantly departing from or defying the family tradition in which they are brought up.

To strengthen the heritage of similarity they see developing in their only child, parents can give that son or daughter the benefit of their mature understanding about the benefits and costs of the trait involved. Sharing of this kind allows the only child an opportunity for vicarious learning from the wisdom of parental experience. Reflecting on what he or she has been told, the child can learn to constructively manage his or her growth.

- Thus, the mother may say: "Like me, you have a lot of interests and love pursuing them all. A lot of interests keeps life from ever getting boring. They make life rich. But I'd like you to know that I have paid a price for keeping up all the varied things I do. I've never committed the time and dedication needed to excel in any one."
- Thus, the father may say: "Like me, you are very quick to speak your mind. And that is good. In general, most people know where you or I stand. They know what we think and feel. But sometimes, speaking up has gotten me in trouble, saying on impulse what on reflection would have been better left unsaid. It's good to speak up, but it's also good to think before you speak. Sometimes I've found it's even good to shut up, to keep reactions and opinions to myself."

3

~~~~~~

RISKS FROM SIMILARITY

"PEER" PRESSURE FROM PARENTS

P arents are a major source of peer pressure on their only son or daughter. Because there are no siblings with whom the only child can affiliate, parents become social peers at home. Not only do they create the ruling norms, they are the child's only alternative for companionship within the family. To be well accepted, the only child (as children do in any peer group) tries to fit in and please the powers that be in order to belong. Like any peer pressure, the kind experienced by the son or daughter in the only child family is partly based on fear.

The price of not fitting in or not going along may be disapproval, criticism, conflict, rejection, or even exclusion. "I still remember the time I criticized my parents for enjoying playing cards. After that, they didn't invite me to join their game anymore, and I felt something was wrong with me." The only child soon discovers that although resemblance to parents is praised and rewarded, sometimes diverging from what they want can cause a temporary loss of good standing. *The problem of having only parents as companions at home is coping with the peer pressure they create.*

This striving for similarity can be costly if the only child suppresses individuality either to court the parents' good opinion or to avoid disappointing them. "Being their only child I was everything to my parents, and they were everything to me. They loved it that I loved what they loved. And when I said I wanted to study what they did, and maybe accomplish some of the things they had, they were delighted. How could I tell them that I really wanted to do something else, to lead an entirely different kind of life from them? What kind of return would that have been after all they've done for me? So I did my best to fit in and follow along."

Many parents of only children do not fully grasp the enormous social influence they have over their son or daughter, or the pressure to conform and please under which that child often secretly labors. Usually it takes the coexistence of multiple children in a family to reduce the "peer pressure" of parents by creating a competing peer group of siblings to which each child also belongs. Now children no longer tend to be compared with their parents but with each other (creating another set of problems from rivalry).

In addition, with multiple children, the exclusive parental attention formerly given the only child becomes diluted, divided among many. No one child any longer remains the parents' sole preoccupation. No one child is always performing on center stage, for good or ill. The increasing influence of siblings on each other gives children alternative models to follow. As individual variation between children becomes apparent, parental tolerance for diversity within the family is increased, and pressure of similarity to parents on any child is reduced.

In the course of normal growth, it can be hard for an only child to honor and assert individuality when it runs counter to how parents are or how they want that child to be. This is why the challenges of adolescence are often so painful for only children (see Part Eight, beginning on page 127).

Many normal adolescent changes can be scary for only children because they cause the boy or girl to deviate from the ruling family norm. It can become difficult

- to rebel against how one was as a child,
- to no longer fit in and conform to family,
- to become more resistant to parental authority,
- to experiment with definitions of identity that parents may disapprove,
- to socially separate from parents in search of independent friendships,
- and to fight for more social freedom than parents may want to give.

In some cases, the fear is so great that the teenager would rather delay adolescence than risk straining the relationship with parents to express the individuality, and to gain the independence, that this period of growth requires.

Because similarity to parents is such a powerful force in the life of only children, it is helpful for parents to be aware of the peer pressure they exert (albeit, usually unintentionally), and to reduce its influence where they can. A few common strategies include:

- Don't praise similarity too highly. ("Good for you, you did it just like us!")
- Don't criticize the child for being different from parents. ("We don't understand how you can listen to such trashy music!")
- Don't punish misdeeds or mistakes with exclusion. ("If that's the way you're going to act, you can spend time by yourself for awhile.")
- Because competition can encourage similarity (causing both parties to contest dominance in a common activity), don't turn a lot of what you do together into a contest. ("Come on, try and beat me if you can!")

- Do let the child know that your acceptance is not conditional on similarity. ("Our love for you doesn't depend on your doing everything like us or liking everything we do.")
- Do be supportive of the only child's diversity. ("Good for you, you did it your way!")
- Do make it clear that most of the differences between you are a source of richness, not divisiveness. ("You teach us by giving us another point of view.")
- When your child is around the age of nine or ten, do forecast some of the adolescent friction that may lay ahead. ("As you begin to want more independence, it's normal for us to go through a period when we have more disagreements over freedom, and you will want to spend more time with friends than family.")

4

~~~~~~

ABSENCE OF SIBLINGS

STRENGTHS FROM BEING
THE ONLY CHILD AT HOME

A child's development is affected by two kinds of influences—those that are present, and those that are absent. Thus, the only child, by *missing out* on having siblings, is influenced both by growing up in a family of adults and by having no other children with whom to interact at home. Both influences can foster strengths in the only child.

Being the exclusive focus of parental love can create a powerful sense of self-importance and support for the only child who becomes sole recipient of all that parents have to offer. Testimony to the advantages of growing up in this kind of family system typically sounds like this: "I loved being an only child. No competition for my parents. No one to be compared with in their eyes. No one to take my things or make me jealous. No need to fight to get my share. I got all my parents had to give." *Within the family, only children can feel very confident and socially secure.*

Another strength is derived from being socialized around adults. Many only children appear both verbally and socially advanced. They may talk very early because they feel encouraged to imitate their parents, and they may develop unusual social poise learning to interact with their parents' adult friends. "How grown-up you are!" is a compliment commonly awarded only children who grow up being taught to act adult by the company they keep. *Only children can be very verbally and socially precocious.*

Building on this social maturity can have decided benefits. The child's unusual poise can give the girl or boy a head start in dealing with the adult social world she or he will someday enter. It is a decided advantage, as a child, to be able to talk comfortably to grown-ups, to confidently approach adult authorities, to be able to discuss wants with those in positions of sufficient responsibility to help.

"If you think you might be interested in newspaper work," suggests the parent, "why don't you call up the editor of our daily paper and see if they have any opportunities for students to get involved?" And the older only child, unlike some peers in multiple-child families who might shy away from such a challenge, does not feel intimidated and goes ahead as suggested. Or the younger only child, used to conversing with parental friends, is encouraged to call one of them up to get an interview for a school project. *Having learned older social skills through socializing with adults, the only child is well equipped to approach the adult world.*

5

~~~~~~

RISKS FROM ABSENCE OF SIBLINGS

DELAYED EMOTIONAL MATURITY

O n the downside, only children can pay a developmental price for the lack of other children in the family. From missing out on the rough and tumble of sibling rivalry, companionship, conflict, and play at home, only children can grow up lacking a degree of *emotional maturity*.

Psychological maturity of any kind is not genetically endowed. It must be earned and learned. It is a gathering of power—of self-understanding, of realistic perspective, and of effective choice. It does not come easy. It comes from hard life experience. *At least at home, the only child lacks exposure to the ups and downs, the give and take, the push and shove of sibling life from which much emotional maturity can be learned.*

Parents tend to be considerate and protective of their only child's feelings. They want to handle any friction between them gently and with care. Not only do they not want their child to come to harm, they themselves do not want to be a source of injury to their beloved. Thus, when disagreements occur, when conflicts arise, when correction must be given, parents of only children tend to be careful about what they say and how they say it. "We go very lightly over the negative because our child is so easily hurt by anything that sounds like criticism in what we say. Since we have such a close relationship, any expression of disapproval from us is deeply felt. And to be honest, it's a two-way street. We want to please our child as much as he wants to please us. So we end up doing our best to be diplomatic so no one gets upset."

Although this protective attitude is understandable, it can prevent robust emotional growth. The more preciously that parents treat their only child, the more they reinforce the notion that he or she is easily bruised or damaged by a strong expression of hard feelings. In consequence, the only child may develop a sense of emotional fragility: "I hate people being mean or rude, and I can't stand conflict."

In this highly sensitized and solicitous relationship, the only child is spared the daily emotional abrasion that tends to characterize relationships between siblings who, in the course of growing up together, often feel free to

- jockey for dominance,
- vie for parental favor,
- tease to put the other down,
- insult to assert verbal dominance,
- fight for who goes first and gets the most,
- exchange hard feelings from daily frustrations,
- argue over differences,
- provoke conflict to get irritations or disappointments out,
- and often allow self-interest and impulse to rule interactions with each other.

Unlike the parent/only child relationship, siblings typically do not feel obliged to act so considerate or careful with each other. Intermittent conflict is usual, hurt feelings happen, people get angry, differences are dealt with directly, and the young combatants usually find a way to reconcile and become good companions soon again.

13

In outside friendships when young, and in love relationships as they grow older, only children sometimes have some emotional catching up to do.

- They may have a low tolerance for frustration and delay of gratification. ("I'm used to getting what I want when I want it.")
- They may take unintentional slights and chance adversity personally. ("I just know this was done on purpose.")
- They may take hurts deeply to heart and hold onto them for a long time. ("It still makes me angry when I think about it.")
- They may only enter significant relationships if they feel that they have sufficient controlling interest to keep them emotionally safe. ("I don't intend to do what is uncomfortable for me.")
- They may be private and protective of vulnerable feelings. ("I don't want to discuss that.")
- They may be inexperienced in working out conflicts to the mutual satisfaction of both parties. ("The only choices are my way, your way, or no way.")

This emotional immaturity is usually remedied through life experience as the child grows older. "It took me years to understand that how my parents and their friends treated me was not a realistic model for what friendship and marriage are meant to be like. As a child, they treated me so considerately I didn't develop any tolerance for emotional give and take. Now I know that sometimes acting upset or being hurt is just part of being in a grown-up relationship."

Although only children can seem socially mature and confident with adults, because of emotional immaturity they can shy away from play relationships with people their own age, preferring either much older or younger company. Should this preference start to become a pattern, parents may need to be assertive about adequately socializing their child's life with groups of other children the same age. Certainly school is one such situation, but often school is not enough. Additional measures may be taken to help the child gather the social experience to emotionally grow up.

- Day care or preschool experiences allow the only child to get some of the rough and tumble feel of being among a group of peers. Having friends over, going over to the homes of friends, being part of a neighborhood group of kids also create valuable exposure. At a preschool age, parents may be his or her preferred company. If so, they may have to initiate these social arrangements against the child's preference. "We can still have time to play together, but I want to you to learn to enjoy playing with other children." The child needs to learn the lessons of friction and friendship that allow emotional growth to occur.

- Sometimes parents may notice certain behaviors in their child when he or she is playing in a group—unwillingness to share or compromise, inability to speak up for himself or take up for herself—that is worth talking about with their only son or daughter at a later time. One responsibility of parents is to explain the world to their child. "Getting along with other people can be hard to do. One way is for each of you to give some so both of you will want to play together. Another is to let the other person know what you like and don't like, because they can't know for sure unless you tell them."

- Within the family, parents can strive to model and encourage the honest sharing of feelings, and not shy away from conflict, but deal with differences in a safe and forthright manner. "When we don't like how you are acting or what you've done, we will tell you how we feel about it. And when you don't like how we are acting or what we've done, we want you to tell us how you feel too. Remember,

15

we can dislike how the other person is acting, and still love each other as much as ever."

If parents treat their only child as emotionally fragile, that is the way the child may expect to be treated by others, and how the child may learn to treat himself or herself.

If parents strive to protect the child from any expression of their occasional hard feelings, or if they disallow the occasional expression of hard feelings from the child, tolerance for emotional negativity and intensity may become diminished to the child's later cost. Parenting is a process of preparation. Protection is an act of prevention. Emotional protectiveness of the kind described can prevent some of the preparation a growing child needs.

6

~~~~~~

THE ONE-PARENT FAMILY

STRENGTHS FROM LIVING WITH A SINGLE PARENT

When abandonment, death, or divorce leaves a parent with sole day-to-day responsibility for an only child, an increased bonding with each other is usually created. Having lost a significant degree of contact with one parent, the only child (particularly if still in elementary school) tends to cling to the one remaining. To provide stability and security, the single parent often grows closer to the child in return. In consequence, a re-bonding of a kind occurs as single parent and only child recommit to the two-person relationship upon which both now depend for nuclear family support. *Roughly one third of only children in this country now live with a single parent,* so this family circumstance is not an uncommon one.

The child may think, or the single parent may actually say: "It's just the two of us now, so we need to stick together." From this mutual reliance, a sense of *partnership* develops from which certain strengths can grow.

In a two-parent household, a lot may be done for the only child. Satisfying his or her desires often becomes a primary focus of parental concern. In a single-parent family, however, indulgence of the only child tends to be qualified by a higher priority—well-being and survival of the family unit. Usually the child is enlisted into partnership to support the family by undertaking more household tasks and initiative for his or her self-care. Awareness of larger family needs is created by these contributions. Compared to the only child in a two-parent family, more work is often demanded by a single parent, less freedom of choice is given, and there is some understanding that the welfare of the family comes before the pleasure of the child.

"Look, I'm the only parent around here. If I put my child on a pedestal and cater to her needs at the expense of our own or my own, the family would collapse. I have to keep my priorities straight: It's me first, we second, and she third. When I'm too tired to do what she wants or what we need at the moment, she's got to let me rest. And when I need her to help out, she does." *For many only children, creation of the single-parent household feels like a promotion and a demotion in family status at the same time. The promotion is being given more responsibility in the family. The demotion is learning to subordinate self-interest and accept less individual importance for the sake of the larger family good.*

Becoming a single parent creates a squeeze: there is more to do, with less adult support to get it all done. In consequence, the single mother or father usually turns to the only child to share more work, to give more help, to take more responsibility, to exercise more independence, to show more consideration, to participate more in family decisions, to do without some of what was previously given, and to do more of what he or she may not necessarily like.

"Everything changed when we lost Dad. I had to grow up in a hurry. I became man of the house because Mom had to depend on me. It was hard, but not all bad. She treated me like my opinions mattered and my help made a difference.

I learned to do a lot and felt good about myself." *Being given more family responsibility at an early age often develops an additional measure of competence and self-esteem.*

Responsibility is taught by parents letting go, risking the child's well-being by giving him or her more freedom of self-regulation or social exposure. Now at the mercy of his or her own decision making, the child is held accountable for consequences of the choices made, taking credit for the good, owning and recovering from the bad. In single-parent households, only children tend to develop more responsibility at an earlier age than their counterparts in two-parent families because more independence is given and more help is needed.

Playing to this strength, single mothers or fathers can make the increased gathering of responsibility a central theme in their parenting by contractually linking it to the growing child's desire for more independence: "I will risk giving you more freedom so long as you keep giving me adequate information about your activities and ongoing evidence of responsible conduct." By the time the more difficult adolescent years arrive, single parents have usually instilled a strong base of responsibility in their only child on which they can depend and trust.

In addition, there is another strength they frequently nurture. From the child's experience of acting as a working partner with the single parent, the only child also learns to become a person who keeps commitments, someone on whom others can rely. This quality tends to stand the boy or girl in good stead in significant relationships, on the job, and in marriage later on.

7

‸‸

RISKS FROM ACTING PARTNER TO THE PARENT

PRESUMING TOO MUCH POWER

Growth is a gathering of power from dependence to independence. Gradually assuming more responsibility is how that power is gained. One risk for the only child is overstepping boundaries of responsibility that have been given. Being a partner is not the same as being an *equal* partner.

Sometimes the single parent needs to clarify the limits of decision making to which the only child is entitled. "Just because I want you to understand and help me think about where our money goes, that doesn't mean you get to choose the way we spend. It's my job to determine what we can afford." The only child needs to understand that input doesn't guarantee outcome, that influence doesn't mean control, that responsibility doesn't mean authority, that adults are not bound by many of the rules a child must live by, and that being a "partner" in the family doesn't entitle him or her to an equal say. *An only child of a single parent can presume more power of responsibility than is appropriate.*

The child's sense of family partnership can get particularly difficult, and serious tensions can arise, when the single parent becomes involved in an adult love relationship, or even decides to remarry. At this point, the mother or father may find the only child acting enemy to this romantic interest. Objects the child: "I don't like him!" "We don't need her!" "He's not family!" "She'll just get in the way!" Partnership with the single parent has caused the only child to become proprietary and feel protective of this relationship, reluctant to allow a potential rival in. In most cases, it is the opposite sex child from the single parent who will feel most threatened, unwilling to yield his or her historical family role of "man" or "woman of the family" to an outsider.

How is the single parent going to dismantle the old partnership with the only child in order to make room for a new spouse? Frustrated with the child's opposition, the mother or father may get angry: "You are not going to keep me from getting married!" Or, emotionally unwilling to deal with the child's unhappiness, the single parent may renege on remarriage: "I just can't marry you since it is so upsetting to my child!"

Neither response is a helpful one. Both refuse to accept and work with the only child's feelings of fear, betrayal, and loss. Better in the first case to assure the child that remarriage will leave the parent's love for the only child unbroken. Better in the second case not to give the child emotionally extortionate power to prevent the parent from another chance at committed adult love. *An only child can grow possessive of his or her relationship with the single parent.*

How can the single parent help the only child keep their partnership in perspective? The answer is, by continually clarifying the child's place in the single parent's world of relationships, and by continually specifying how much the child can and cannot decide.

For example, any time more freedom of responsibility is given (the only child is allowed to begin a part-time job), the single parent can make the *limits* of unilateral and shared decision making clear. "*I* will decide where you can work and if you can work, grades permitting. *We* will decide how much of what you earn goes into savings and how many hours a week you work. And *you* will decide how to spend the money you don't save and how you conduct yourself on the job."

To keep an only child from becoming unduly possessive of the single parent, it helps for the mother or father to insist on a separate social life of his or her own. "Going out is my decision. I love being with you, but I also want adult companionship for friendship. I want to keep open the possibility of a romantic relationship, perhaps one day even of remarriage. I promise that if any social relationship I have becomes serious, I will let you know, and you will have time to get to know that person. Should we decide to marry, there will still be enough of my love to go around. You will always be my child, and all three of us together will work out whatever new adjustments are required for us to become a family."

It is also a good idea for the mother or father to maintain an active social circle for three additional reasons:

1. The child needs to know that he or she is *not* the parent's major *social companion* (or else the child may restrict his or her social life for the sake of the parent).
2. The child needs to know that he or she is *not* the parent's major *personal confidant* (or else the child becomes overloaded by the adult's emotional dependence).
3. The child needs to know that the parent is not the only source of *social support* (or else the child has no other adult backup in case of emergencies.)

8

✦✦✦

THE TWO-PARENT FAMILY

STRENGTHS FROM FEELING ONE OF THREE

Adding a second child to a family can be a painful transition for parents who must give up their exclusive infatuation with number one to make loving room for number two. Now they must decide which child gets the first response when both are clamoring for attention. Sometimes hard choices must be made about which child is most in need. Having to divide their attention between the children often brings a sense of internal conflict, insufficiency, and guilt that parents did not suffer when they had only one. "We just can't give to two all we gave to one. So now our oldest gets less, and our second doesn't get as much as we once gave the first."

There is a sense of parental luxury with an only child. Parents don't have to worry about providing for one at the expense of another, or having to fairly divide resources between contesting children. Parents can continue to indulge their preoccupation with the child who has brought them together in a new way. Before the child, they were just married as partners, as wife and husband. Now they have become married as parents, as mother and father. *Because the only child has birthed them into parenthood, he or she is often treated as part of the adult union.*

Strengthened by so much undivided love, the first and only child can feel undivided from the parents, part of the marital love that unites them all. Mother and father treat the child as "one of us," as an integral part of their new relationship as parents. When a second child comes along, this treatment generally changes as both children are treated as "two of *them*," the first child now becoming just "one of the kids."

If in a single-parent home, the only child can feel like a co-member on the team that keeps the family going, in a two-parent home, a sense of belonging in the relationship between mother and father can cause the only child to feel part of the parental marriage. "Particularly when I was a young child, there wasn't much social distinction made between my parents and me. They were linked to me and I was linked to them. I always felt attended to by one of them or the other. As I grew old enough to have opinions, I was consulted in family decisions. I rarely felt left out. If they were sitting on the couch, I snuggled in between. If they were talking, I was made part of the conversation. If they went off to do something, they usually took me along. I was really made to feel a part of them. I guess if you had asked me about their marriage, I probably would have said it included me in the middle."

The strengths from marital belonging for the only child are significant.

- There is an enormous sense of *security* that comes from being so deeply anchored in the parental relationship.
- There is a sense of *intimacy* that allows the child to feel deeply known and to deeply know the parents.
- There is a sense of *equity* with parents that encourages the child to be outspoken and not be intimidated by their adult authority.
- There is an experience of *inclusion* in parental conversations, in parental social relationships, in parental activities

outside the home that provides the child with enormous exposure to the adult world.

This sense of belonging is esteem building when it gives the child a sense of adult status, and it is problematic when the boy or girl forgets that he or she is still a child. One challenge for parents is to provide the child with enough social and play experience with age-mates so that he or she doesn't pass up normal childhood development with peers for the company of adults. Another is not to place the child on such an adult level that he or she becomes "bossy" to live with: "I have as much right to decide what goes on in this family as you do!" No, the boy or girl doesn't. Parents are the adults. He or she is the child.

9

~~~~~~

RISKS FROM FEELING PART OF THE MARRIAGE

BECOMING CAUGHT IN THE MIDDLE

The security from feeling firmly placed in the middle of a loving parental marriage can turn to anxiety when parents do not get along. Now the only child, intimately acquainted with the relationship between her mother and father, and highly emotionally attuned to both, feels caught in the middle of their tensions and conflicts with each other.

When the marriage feels unhappy, the only child can feel insecure. "It was the worst part of my growing up. Although my parents both loved me, they didn't love each other. It was excruciating. I was the only family happiness they had. The pain they felt with each other became my pain. Sometimes I even wondered if it was my fault. Were they just staying together for me? I did everything I knew to help make their marriage work, and when my efforts came to nothing, I felt I had failed the two people I loved. There was this pressure to take one parent's side against the other, and sometimes one would even use me to get back at the other. Their fighting just tore me up."

The downside of intimacy with parents is the only child's sensitivity to disharmony between them, and a tendency to take responsibility for trying to put the marriage right. Most painful of all, an only child can get placed in the middle between opposing parents.

- The child can be used as a *weapon*. A parent can claim the only child's loyalty against the other parent: "We don't know how you can call yourself a responsible father and come home drunk this way."
- The child can be used as a *pawn*. A parent can enlist the only child in a manipulation "to get" the other parent: "Talk to your mother if you want to know why we're out of money."
- The child can be used as a *mediator*. Parents can enlist the child in solving their marital problems: "See if you can get your father (or your mother) to forgive me."

An only child cannot be pulled into alliance with one parent in the marriage without at the same time becoming estranged from the other parent.

Problems that arise from marital belonging have to do with inadequate *distinctions* and *separations* being made by the parents with their only child. In words and actions, what needs to be communicated is this:

- "We three make up a family." (Togetherness is affirmed.)
- "We two make up a marriage." (Separateness of the parental union is declared.)
- "We two are the grown-ups." (The adult/child distinction is made.)
- " You are our child." (Parental commitment is affirmed.)
- "Our job is to take care of you; it is not your job to take care of us." (Assignment of responsibility is clarified.)

Certainly there are a number of actions that parents, when unhappy with each other, can *avoid* for the sake of their only child.

1. Don't use the child as an emotional refuge or support when not getting along with each other. ("Well, at least my child loves me.")
2. Don't blame the child for marital conflict. ("We are arguing because of you.")
3. Don't ask the child to take sides. ("Who do you think is right?")
4. Don't complain about the other parent to the child. ("He never does what he promises." "She never gets things right.")
5. Don't compare the child to the other parent in negative ways. ("You're stubborn just like your mother." "You have a temper just like your father.")

None of these suggestions means that parents of an only child must always get along. That is an unrealistic expectation. Every marriage has its normal ups and downs. At issue is how to manage these inevitable tensions, upsets, and conflicts so that the only child doesn't feel in jeopardy, doesn't feel caught in the middle, doesn't feel at fault, doesn't feel responsible for making things better.

To this end, perhaps as early as age six depending on the maturity of the child, parents may want to say something to him or her like this: "We want you to know that sometimes in our marriage we will not get along. That is true of all marriages. Because we are all so close, you will probably sense when there is some tension between us. Always feel free to ask: 'Is something wrong?' If there is, we will answer honestly so you won't feel you are just imagining. Then we will want some private time just with each other to work out the problem. What the problem is will be our business, but when we have worked it out we will tell you, because that is part of what you need to know."

10

∧∧∧

EXCLUSIVE ATTENTION

STRENGTHS FROM BEING IN THE SPOTLIGHT

"**S**ometimes it felt like growing up under a microscope, my parents observing every little way I was, noticing every little thing I did. The good part was feeling I really had their attention. I never felt ignored or neglected. The bad part was there was no escape. If anything was slightly wrong, they picked up on it right away. 'Is something the matter?' they would ask. And usually there was, because they knew me so well."

There is a quality of attention that parents give their first and only child that no subsequent children get. Part infatuation and part anxiety, first-time parents (and this can include remarried couples parenting together for the first time) tend to fall in love with parenting, the creation of family, and the miracle of their only child. At the same time, they take their new responsibility very seriously. Cautious, careful, sensitive, hovering, protective, they are often inclined to seek medical advice at the infant's earliest sign of discomfort. First-time parents are more concerned and less confident, more worried and less relaxed, than seasoned parents who have had children before. In multiple-child families, later children tend to become less wonderful and less worrisome as parents reap the benefits of past parenting experience.

The historical data really tells the difference. On first and only children, all kinds of records, photographs, and artifacts are usually meticulously maintained, evidence of the close attention parents gave. Keeping such treasures shows how treasured the only child is, all first children being only children for awhile. On subsequent children, this data is less completely and consistently kept.

"Listen to me!" "Let me show you!" "Look at what I've done!" "Watch what I've learned to do!" In response to these requests from their first or only child for attention, parents respond with true delight. The quality of response they give is usually extremely positive, noticing, and supportive.

The only child is a *trial child*. This means that he or she is the one on whom mother and father get to try out their parenting skills and develop their parenting strategies *for the first time*. To keep the child comfortable, to influence the child to comply, to get the child to cooperate, all take a lot of trial and error. There is a distinctly experimental feel to what they do and the name of that feeling is *anxiety*. Troubled by not knowing what to do, parents are much more inclined to read parenting books for their first child than for those that follow. They tend to be receptive to "advice from an expert."

An only child can sometimes sense this parental anxiety, actually incorporating their fear of making mistakes into her or his own decision making. "I think the reason I'm so cautious and concerned about not messing up is because that's how my parents are with me. They are very careful in their parenting, and that's the way I've learned to treat myself."

People pay attention to what *matters* to them. In the case of an only child, parents pay a lot of attention because the only son or daughter matters to them so much. Literally and symbolically, this constant flow of attention gives evidence to the child of her or his importance in the parents' eyes, creating three powerful outcomes for the child:

1. From this continuing statement of worth from parents, the only child gathers a continuing sense of self-worth.
2. From the close notice parents give, the only child becomes closely noticing of himself or herself.
3. From the approving audience that parents happily provide, the only child learns to put himself or herself forward to be noticed, at least at home.

Attention counts for a lot. Ask a group of fourth- or fifth-graders if they would rather be teased and name-called or be ignored and excluded, and most would choose being teased and name-called. Why? Because "bad attention feels better than no attention at all." Getting attention means that your presence is being counted, that others are investing energy in relationship to you, that, for good or ill, they find your presence worth acknowledging.

Even only children, should they feel frustrated in getting the immediate attention they want, may resort to tactics that provoke a negative kind. Impatient to tell about school, and feeling frustrated that the parent is busy talking on the phone, the child picks up the extension in the next room and interrupts the conversation: "I want to tell you what happened in class today!" By getting mad at this misbehavior, the parent gives the child bad attention, but that is preferred by the boy or girl to the absence of attention he or she was receiving before. (Delay of gratification when attention is desired can be hard to learn for some indulged only children.)

To nurture strengths from attention in their only child, parents can make sure to *diversify* the kinds of attention they give, each of the great variety signifying a different cause for valuing the child's worth. A few of the more common kinds include:

- *Listening and replying* signify that the child is worth hearing. ("In answer to what you said, here is what I think.")
- *Watching and noticing* signify that the child is worth being observed. ("We love seeing you perform.")
- *Assisting and encouraging* signify that the child is worth being helped. ("I'll give you a hand, try again.")
- *Expressing interest and curiosity* signify that the child is worth being known. ("Tell me some more.")
- *Supervising and correcting* signify that the child is worth taking care of. ("We won't stand by and let you hurt yourself.")

The more variety of attention that parents give, the more broadly based does the child's sense of self-worth become.

Finally, from receiving so much positive parental attention, the only child learns to enjoy paying positive attention to himself or herself. He or she learns the art of keeping oneself good company. Time alone is usually good time. Rarely bored, the only child develops many ways to occupy himself or herself and be content. Those who marry an only child often see the outcome of this capacity for self-absorption. The only child spouse usually likes keeping a certain amount of separateness in the relationship so he or she can enjoy precious time alone.

11

RISKS FROM EXCLUSIVE ATTENTION

THE DANGER OF EXCESSIVE WORRY

An only child represents an enormous investment for parents. Because all their parenting is wrapped up in the one child, the attention they bring to their mothering and fathering can be fraught with *worry*. They have so much to lose. They fear making the wrong decisions for the child, inflicting unintentional harm, or exposing him or her to excessive risk. They fear the child becoming victim of his or her own impulsive or unwise decisions. They fear the adverse influence of other children. They fear chance circumstance striking their child down. There is so much to fear and so little they control, it is easy to give in to a tyranny of fear: "We don't how we'd survive if anything happened to our child!"

In such a state of worry, nervous parents can convey that fear to a sensitive and impressionable only child, scaring him or her away from accepting some of the normal challenges of growing up. "I'd rather stay home than go to the party with my friends." Parents of an only child can be overprotective, and when they are, the child can learn to be overcautious in response. The child can sacrifice healthy risk taking to his or her own exaggerated worries about personal safety. *Whereas affirmative attention from parents tends to enhance self-worth, their anxious attention can erode self-confidence and retard independent growth.*

Constructive and Destructive Worry

The key to moderating fearful attention with their child is learning to distinguish between *constructive* and *destructive worry*. Constructive worry is *proactive parenting.* Recognizing that a normal part of being a child is acting without always first considering the risks, parents try to increase the child's vision of harmful possibilities by saying something like this. "Because we don't want to send you blindly into a new situation you have never experienced, we want you to think about an important question: *What if?* We want to explore with you some possible problems that might arise. And then we want you to come up with some contingency plans just in case any of these difficulties should occur."

By using constructive worry, parents teach their only child to stop and think ahead. Knowing that this forethought is in place often reduces the amount of anxiety parents feel, and they are able to send their child off into some new experience supported by their confidence and not burdened by their fears.

Destructive worry can lead to *compulsive overparenting* where parents drive themselves and their only child crazy with excessive needs for control. Parents can *chain worry:* "If you flunk this class then maybe you'll flunk others, then maybe you'll drop out of school, and then maybe you'll end up living on the street!" Parents can ask *crazy questions* (questions for which there are no answers): "How do you know for sure you won't get hit by a drunk driver and get killed?" Parents can *obsessively control:* "You're not going out unless you check in with us by phone every half hour." Compulsive overparenting invokes strategies for safety that only worsen parental fear.

If parents ever find themselves crossing the line that separates constructive from destructive worry, they can reduce the tendency to compulsively overparent by:

- trying to confine their worries to the near future, and not chain worry into a far distant time;
- trying to interrupt the flow of crazy questions by only allowing those for which sensible answers exist;
- and trying to let go what cannot realistically be controlled.

They can also make three requests of the child:

1. *Try to think ahead.* Anticipate the complexities and consequences of what you want to do. ("Before you build a Roller Derby car to race, I want you tell me some of the safe-driving skills you will need to know.")
2. *Keep us informed.* If you are out and change your plans, please let us know. ("If at one friend's home you both decide to visit the home of another, please ask us first.")
3. *Call us should you get in trouble or so you can stay out of trouble.* ("If your friends are planning a prank you don't want to be a part of, make an excuse, call us, and we'll come get you, no questions asked.")

12

~~~~~~

THE "ONLY" ATTITUDE

STRENGTHS FROM BEING FULL OF ONESELF

From all the affirmative parental attention they receive, only children tend to become full of themselves. Flourishing under the exclusive focus of parental love, only children tend to develop a strong sense of self-love and self-esteem. Being so full of themselves can create an "only" attitude that can be empowering in a number of ways.

Four strengths from being full of themselves can serve only children well.

1. *Fullness of self encourages a focus on self-satisfaction.* Many only children tend to be very self-directed, dedicated to becoming involved in interests and activities that personally matter to them, able to initiate that involvement on their own. "I love to read when I get home from school, so my parents let me have this time alone."

2. *Fullness of self encourages a focus on future for self.* Many only children, from a very young age, start thinking about what they want to do in the years ahead. Part of taking themselves seriously is taking their future seriously by creating personal goals they want to pursue. "I've already thought about what I want to study when I get to college, even though college is still six years away."

3. *Fullness of self encourages expression of self.* Many only children seek creative outlets to give expressive form to who and how they are. There is the sense of wanting to express themselves because they feel they have something personally worth saying. "When I am dancing, I am performing Me."

4. *Fullness of self encourages social independence of self.* Many only children, secure in their relationship with parents, liking a few friends but not in dire need of them, and happy spending time alone with themselves, feel free from worry about social scrutiny. The possibility of social disapproval from "the eyes of the world" does not bother them. They lead their lives according to what personally matters, not by first considering whether it pleases other people. "It's not that I don't care what other people think about me; it's just that what they think is less important than what I think about myself."

To support this fullness of self in their only child, parents can offer four kinds of support in response.

- *To support self-satisfaction:* if the child wants, give sufficient time and space at home for him or her to cultivate those interests and activities that personally matter.
- *To support future for self:* if the child wants, help get advance information about occupational interest or career choice, special training or college preparation. Even arrange for contacts where the child could interview someone doing what the girl or boy is considering some day choosing.
- *To support expression of self:* if the child wants, get instruction and provide an appreciative audience for his or her particular avenue of creative development.

- *To support social independence of self:* if the child wants assurance, give permission for him or her to follow an individual path even when it sometimes means not fitting in with peers.

The "only" attitude often causes the only child in later years to retain a capacity for self-absorption, self-knowledge, self-companionship, and self-development that can all make for a rich and rewarding journey through adult life.

13

RISKS FROM THE "ONLY" ATTITUDE

BECOMING SELF-CENTERED TO A FAULT

The harmful effects of being full of oneself can occur when the only child starts assuming too much self-importance in the family, and parents (unwilling to disappoint or cross their precious son or daughter) allow this unhealthy growth to continue. Fullness of self, if allowed to flourish with no concern for others in the family, can cause the only child to acquire an "only" attitude that is self-centered to a fault.

- "My way is the only way."
- "My needs come first."
- "My vote counts most."
- "My opinion is always right."
- "My rules are how we play."
- "My feelings should be first considered."
- "My terms must be met."
- "My wants must be gratified."
- "My welfare before others."
- "My happiness is number one."
- "Me before we."

By agreeing when they don't really agree, by sacrificing healthy self-interest, by giving in, by backing off, by deferring, by not speaking up, by not taking stands, by avoiding conflict, parents can encourage the only child's "only" attitude to develop into a tyranny of self within the family. Even worse, eventually they send out into the world a young adult who believes that this is how roommate, employment, or caring relationships should work.

Then being a "spoiled" child becomes unveiled for what it really means: *learning self-centered conduct in childhood that spoils the development of healthy adult relationships later on.* Now the only child discovers that a one-way model of relationship doesn't work very well out in the real world, and must learn the skills of two-way relationships through hard experience.

If parents can keep in mind that one purpose of family is to serve as a sheltered experience in which they approximate the larger social reality the child will one day enter, then they can teach the interpersonal skills the child will one day need to cope successfully with independence. *The way for parents to moderate the risks of the "only" attitude is to teach the only child the principles of mutuality.*

Mutuality means learning to live in relationships in a way that serves the needs of all parties, not just one. To varying degrees, depending upon how parents catered to his or her needs growing up, the only child may lack experience with the three important interpersonal skills upon which mutuality is based.

1. *Reciprocity* is the understanding that in all healthy relationships there needs to be an exchange such that each party not only derives some benefit from the other's giving, but also gives so others enjoy some benefit in return. Thus, parents need to let the only child know that family relationships need to be two-way, not just one. Just as they want to give to their child in ways that feel good to him or her, so they want comparable giving in return.

2. *Sensitivity* is exercised by realizing that through family intimacy, members learn a lot about each other's vulnerabilities. Out of consideration for this understanding, all parties resolve not to act in ways that knowingly will cause each other hurt. Just as they, when frustrated in conflict, do not strike out in anger to deliberately hurt their child, so they expect the only child to exercise the similar restraint with them.

3. *Compromise* requires that sometimes when differences arise, each family member, for the larger good of getting along, will put some self-interest aside to reach an agreement that partly satisfies the other person's wants. This agreement supports the common interest both have in the ongoing well-being of the relationship. Compromise means being willing to be satisfied with less than 100 percent of what each person ideally wants. It means giving some to get some. Just as parents don't always demand that it's going to be their way or else, or their way or no way, so they expect the child to be flexible when working out differences with them. Finding our way creates a middle ground.

Learning mutuality can moderate some of the self-centered tendencies in the only child that can develop when the boy or girl, as a function of inadequately demanding parenting, gets too full of himself or herself.

14

SELF-IMAGE

STRENGTHS FROM A POSITIVE PERCEPTION

One of the good parts of the *special valuing* (being treated as an exceptionally special person) that only children get at home is believing that the rave reviews from their adoring parents are true. In consequence, these children tend to construct a very positive image of themselves based on the loving feedback they constantly receive.

Just as affirmative attention nourishes self-esteem, so special valuing *shapes self-image*. In this respect, parental attention acts like a mirror of response in which the only child sees his or her reflection. "Mirror, mirror, on the wall, who's the fairest of them all?" asks the queen in *Snow White*. When an only child asks this question of his or her image reflected in parental eyes, the answer is often a resounding: "Me!"

It is important for parents to be mindful of the power of the estimate they routinely give: "You did great!" "You're wonderful!" "You can do anything!" What the child does not realize is that this may be the voice of infatuation or wish fulfillment speaking. The child's image is in danger of becoming distorted through the eyes of parents who sincerely believe, or want to believe, that their one and only child's ordinary accomplishments are a miracle of exceptional achievement. Without another child to whom they can compare their first, it is hard for parents not to occasionally overreact and lose realistic perspective. "Nobody," explained a parent, "who has an only child believes they have just an average child." That statement is probably correct. Also true is that few only children start out life being willing to consider themselves only average.

It is extremely psychologically important for any child, not just an only child, to see himself or herself in a positive light. *Self-image can dictate feelings and motivate actions that tend to confirm children's pictures of themselves.* In simplest terms, parents who are never satisfied no matter how hard their son or daughter struggles to please (because they believe criticism motivates achievement) can unwittingly cause the child to think of himself or herself as inadequate. Feeling hopeless, the child can gradually give up trying, thereby reinforcing the self-image of failure to which he or she has become painfully wed.

Conversely, parents who reward effort as well as outcome (because they believe without striving there can be no accomplishment) can encourage the child to think of himself or herself as persistent. Feeling determined, the child keeps trying in the face of adversity, thereby reinforcing the image of tenacity that he or she feels proud to claim. *What parental attention reflects to their child about their child has some power of self-fulfilling prophecy for their child.*

Because of the amount of positive response parents routinely give, the only child is encouraged to develop positive self-regard. In consequence, only children often tend to:

- consider themselves *capable* and feel confident *pursuing ambitious goals;*
- consider themselves *intelligent* and feel comfortable defending and *asserting their opinion;*
- consider themselves *valuable* and insist on *being well-treated.*

Evaluative or Descriptive Feedback

Helpful ways for parents to strengthen the affirmative self-image of their only child are to keep their feedback *descriptive* and *not evaluative, realistic* and *not idealistic.*

By giving *evaluative feedback*, parents judge *how well* a child is acting or achieving by expressing their degree of approval. In doing so, they convey more information about how they are feeling ("We're so proud of you!") than about what exactly they are responding to in the child's character or conduct. Evaluative feedback is not very informative for the child who knows that the parents are pleased, but learns little else.

In contrast, by giving *descriptive feedback*, parents specify *what about* the child that has caught the parent's positive attention. "I enjoy watching the way you make friends laugh with your sense of humor." From this parental reflection, the child comes away with more appreciation for the funny part of who he or she is.

Idealistic or Realistic Feedback

By giving *idealistic feedback*, parents allow their enthusiasm and love for the child to drive their response to positive extremes. "Nobody could have done it better!" "Keep this up and you'll be famous one day!" In doing so, they can create an image of exceptionality on which the child is encouraged to build unrealistic self-expectations.

In contrast, by giving *realistic feedback*, parents anchor the child's self-perception in the actual world by including some sense of relative standing with peers. "Like most of your teammates, you played hard throughout the whole game, good for you!" "The high test score shows that you did better than about 80 percent of other students, and some 20 percent even outscored you. You did very well!" It can be helpful when parents give affirmative feedback to frame their response so that the child gets a realistic sense of his or her own merits relative to others.

15

~~~~~~

RISKS FROM SELF-IMAGE

THE DISTORTION FROM BELIEVING ONE IS SPECIAL

"**E**ntering kindergarten was probably the biggest shock of my life. At home, there had been no competition and no comparison. I came first and no one was better than me. Then suddenly, as one of twenty-some kids, I wasn't the most important anymore. Even worse, I was nowhere near as special as I thought I was. What a comedown!"

School is often the first major change of social reference many only children experience outside of family. It is the first chance they get to be treated as one of many and to reevaluate their social standing within a community of peers. To the degree that special valuing received at home has encouraged unrealistic thinking about themselves, they may bring an inflated self-image to school. This inflated self-image may not fit the reaction given by the other children, the teacher, or their new experience of themselves. For only children, adjusting to school can sometimes demand significant self-reappraisal.

- There can be a sense of fraud: "I'm not so special after all!"
- There can be a sense of betrayal: "I'm not as smart as my parents told me I was!"

- There can be a sense of disappointment: "I'm not measuring up to what is expected of me!"
- There can be a sense of futility: "What's the point of trying if the best I can do is not as good as a lot of other students?"

Only children who enter school with an inflated self-image may need some help coming to terms of acceptance with the new picture of how special and capable they really are. The first help parents can give is not to make a hard social adjustment worse by trying to replicate at school the sense of special treatment the child receives at home.

- Don't try to bend the rules and get exceptions made so the child receives special treatment not accorded other students.
- Don't rationalize to the child or blame the school for the child's unwillingness to follow rules, to successfully socialize with other students, or to complete assigned work on time.

Some only children, as a function of being indulged as the center of attention at home, may not have learned the *Three Social C's* for coping well with school—*Conformity* (fitting in to get along), *Compliance* (obeying to get along), and *Cooperation* (working with others to get along). If this is the case, parents can tutor the child about these realities by explaining that school life doesn't work exactly the same as home life.

They can also explain to the child that simply because they think he or she is wonderful, the outside world may not be equally impressed. In addition, they can tell the child that he or she does not have to earn the same response at school to continue to receive parental love and approval at home.

They might consider saying to the child something like this: "When you start school, you will be one among a large group of children, all equally important to the teacher. When you do your work, you will find that you will do better than some students and not as well as others. That is to be expected. You do not have to be the best student to do okay. If you try hard and do all your work and still come out around the middle—average—that is good enough. Remember, being average and ordinary is the way most of us are most of the time."

The purpose of giving a message like this is to prepare the child to enter school with a self-image that fits the realistic experience and treatment that he or she is likely to receive in the more complex social world of school.

16

ATTACHMENT

STRENGTHS FROM HOLDING ON

In human relationships, the more intense the attachment (a couple in love, for example), the more difficult the separations (they often cannot bear to be apart). Conversely, the greater the sense of separation (a span of fifteen years between an oldest and youngest child, for example), the more difficult meaningful attachment becomes (they find little common ground on which to meet).

Between these two contrasting states in relationships, parents and the only child tend to have more experience and do better with attachment than with separation. Holding on feels more familiar and easier than letting go. Thus, the great challenges of parenting an only child often occur at three major separation points.

1. When the child leaves the sanctuary of home for the first time and enters the larger, unprotected institution of school, he or she begins the separation into a larger world (around ages five to six).
2. When the child enters adolescence and begins rebelling out of childhood, he or she starts the social separation from parents and family (around ages nine to thirteen).
3. When the older adolescent moves out on his or her own during trial independence, he or she begins the separation from home (around ages eighteen to twenty-three).

Because the attachment has been so strong, these separations can be hard to make both for parents and only children. The little child may be reluctant to leave the security of parents for the challenges of school. The early adolescent may be reluctant to push against and pull away from parents and begin to assert social independence. The older adolescent may be reluctant to leave the security of home for the insecurity of living on one's own. Separation for parents and only children can be hard to do. The capacities for both attachment and separation are required, however, if parents are going to encourage the child to learn dependence (from attachment) and independence (from separation).

It is through affirmative attention, constantly given, that only children become attached to parents who are the primary love-givers and caretakers in their lives. Being the exclusive focus of parental attention, only children tend to become extremely attached to parents who are extremely absorbed in them. From this powerful bonding, the only child is usually blessed with a deep sense of security and trust. This is the birthright of most only children and it is invaluable. *This strong sense of dependence on parents provides the foundation for the development of a strong independence as the child grows.*

Taking for granted his or her solid reliance on parents as a base from which to grow, the only child feels free to invest energy in his or her own independent self-development. *Strong attachment to parents typically begets strong commitment to self-interest.* Characteristics that commonly testify to the only child's self-attachment include:

- *Certainty*—knowing himself or herself well enough to be very sure of personal likes, opinions, and beliefs;
- *Willfulness*—commitment to insist on what he or she wants and to resist what he or she doesn't want;

- *Outspokenness*—willingness to speak up for himself or herself when differences with parents or other authorities arise;
- *Sufficiency*—ability to enjoy his or her own solitary company.

Well-attached only children often display a quality of self-assurance that reflects the security they feel within themselves and with their parents.

Because most human characteristics are double-edged, having both beneficial and harmful potentials, even strengths have their downsides. Parents often find a self-involved and assertive only child hard to handle. "We didn't know when we encouraged him to speak his mind that we were training him to argue with us later on." "We didn't know when we supported the interests she loves that she would become so intolerant of doing what she doesn't like."

The dilemma for many parents is how to contain their only child's strengths without injuring his or her tenacious spirit. There are some strategies that can be helpful in accomplishing this compromise.

- When the child speaks with absolute conviction about what is right and true (*certainty*), don't try to argue him or her out of this belief if you are convinced that the child is wrong or mistaken. It often works better to accept what the child says, disagree without correcting him or her, and state your own alternative point of view. "We respect your opinion, but we see the situation differently and here is why." Clearly counter the child's belief with your own.
- When the child becomes obstinate about what he or she does or does not want to do (*willfulness*), don't immediately threaten, punish, or engage in a power struggle by resorting to superior force to win at all costs. Instead, patiently wait the child out, using relentless pursuit to

wear the opposition down. "We know you don't want to, but we shall keep after you and after you and after you until you get your chores done." Use insistence to wear the child's resistance down.

- When the child argues over an unpopular parental stand (*outspokenness*), don't shut him or her down by treating speaking up as disrespectful talking back. Instead, hear the child out so he or she has a chance to get his or her frustration out. "We will listen to your complaints, but you need to know we probably won't change our minds." Make a compromise: the child can have his or her say, and then parents can get their way.
- When the child wants to be solitary (*sufficiency*), don't treat this as an antisocial or unfriendly act. Appreciate the child's capacity for his or her own companionship and self-directed play. "We're glad you can enjoy time alone." The foundation for contentment is liking oneself.

17

RISKS FROM ATTACHMENT

PROBLEMS OF DEPENDENCY

When attachment between parents and the only child becomes an end in itself, and separation is mutually resisted out of fear of loss, then problems of dependency can develop in childhood that tend to worsen by the end of adolescence.

- The older adolescent may still depend for *identity* on similarity to parents. ("To be who I am, I must be like how they are.")
- The older adolescent's self-acceptance may still depend on *approval* from parents. ("Unless I please them, I can't feel good about myself.")
- The older adolescent's well-being may still depend on parental *support*. ("My parents must be there to take care of me.")
- The older adolescent may still depend for primary *companionship* on the company of parents. ("My parents are the only friends I need.")

For the only child, security comes from two sources: feeling safe when attached to parents, and feeling safe when separated from parents. Dependently attached only children may lack the second source of safety.

Given the risks of attachment described above, parents might want to consider four strategies for reducing their likelihood of occurrence.

1. Give permission for the child's individuality even when it means significant dissimilarity from parents. ("We have never been athletic, but we are glad you are. Differences between us provide more to share and appreciate about each other.")

2. Give the child permission for satisfying self even when it means displeasing parents. ("We don't always have to like the choices that you make, any more than you always have to like the choices we make. We can dislike how each other acts sometimes and still love each other.")

3. Give the child permission for self-care responsibility, even when it means parents are no longer needed. ("The more you learn to do for yourself, the less help from us you'll need. Just because we are no longer taking care of you doesn't mean we won't always care about you.")

4. Give the child permission for putting time with friends ahead of time with parents. ("We always love being with you, but we know that family are no substitute for the kind of fun and closeness you can have with friends. Only with friends can you share what it feels like to be a young person now.")

It takes practice for parents and the only child to get used to separation from and independence of each other. When the boy or girl is young, coming to trust that they can still remain securely emotionally connected when separated affirms that there is no loss of attachment when they are apart.

Letting go is often the hardest when the only child graduates from adolescence into adulthood. Because the child has been such a central focus in the parents' life, letting go may feel to them like losing the child forever and being left alone. "The empty nest" may temporarily feel like a place of abandonment. Yet, parents who are unable to let go risk disabling the grown-up child who may hold on to them in return. Consequently, he or she may have difficulty making independent attachments, managing self-support, and accepting individual responsibility.

An extreme example of this inability to let go is an attachment trap to which some mothers of only children can fall prey. Emotional and physical entrancement with a help-less infant child can be absorbing for any first-time mother. It is common, and in some ways functional, for this attachment to become primary for awhile, as many husbands may notice: "My wife is more caught up with the baby than she is concerned with me."

Often, this period of intense attachment to the infant is extended through the entrancing first few years of being a toddler, when the mother/child bond can grow extremely deep and become extremely mutually satisfying. Then, as the weaned child grows more independent, as maternal infatua-tion gradually wanes, the primary intimacy of marriage reasserts itself and attachment to the child is put into a more separated sense of perspective.

In multiple-child families, it is the arrival of the second child that often helps break the magical hold of child number one, who can experience a significant loss as maternal atten-tion necessarily shifts to care for the new brother or sister. Without benefit of an additional child, however, a few mother/only child relationships can continue primarily attached throughout the boy's or girl's growing up. The spe-cial quality of the relationship remains unrivaled by the mother's husband or by significant relationships the older child makes. In consequence, a parental marriage and a young person's capacity to make an independent commitment in love can both become disabled.

It is possible for a mother to love too much. It is possible for her to be unwilling to discharge her final, painful responsibility of parenting—accepting that all parenting must ultimately end in loss because the greater loving is to let the loved one go.

18

~~~~~~

INTIMACY

STRENGTHS FROM EMOTIONAL CLOSENESS

To say that parents and their only child tend to be close seems to belabor the obvious. How could it be otherwise? So much affection, so much focus from and on each other, creates a degree of bonding that is not disrupted or distracted by siblings. The closeness they feel is rooted in spending much time together, caring a lot for each other, and coming to know each other very well.

Mindful of the only child's well-being, parents remain close for security and comfort. Testifying to this empowering attachment, the child may declare: "I can always count on my parents being there for me."

Unmindful of the risks that excessive attachment brings, however, they can get too close for comfort. Testifying to this debilitating sense of closeness, the child may declare: "It's like we've always lived in the same emotional space. We each feel each other's feelings just like they are our own." Keeping the degree of emotional attachment within constructive bounds means mixing a sense of togetherness for commonality with a sense of separateness for individuality so that, in the poet's words, "the pillars of the temple stand apart." *The only child needs to feel part of the family, but not part of the parents.*

The great strength of closeness from the attachment between parents and the only child is the quality of intimacy that can grow up between them. Through sensitive observation and honest conversation, they come to understand a lot about each other. Assuming this intimacy is handled constructively, at the end of adolescence, the young man or woman is able to achieve four degrees of separation:

1. Although still sensitive to their well-being, he or she is *emotionally detached* from parents.
2. Although still sharing a lot in common with them, he or she is *psychologically differentiated* from parents.
3. Although still by love connected to parents, he or she is capable of being *intimately committed* in other relationships of value.
4. And although still the beneficiary of their past support, he or she is *socially independent* from parents.

Communication skills of deeply sharing, deeply sensing, and deeply listening that have often been learned with parents can well equip the only child for satisfying intimacy with friends and other loved ones as an adult *if the risks of intimacy have been safely managed in the family.*

The Risks of Intimacy

Expressing one's inner thoughts and feelings, exposing one's frailties and failings, and openly expressing dislikes and disagreements all demand trust and often require courage in any relationship. For the only child, however, concerned about retaining the good opinion of parents, these kinds of self-disclosure can be daunting. Those we love the most can cause us to feel the best, or hurt us the worst, because we are most vulnerable to their approval and disapproval, acceptance and rejection.

To nurture intimacy, parents need to show the child that they are committed to keeping intimacy safe. This means that parents avoid using sensitive knowledge gained from what the trusting child has disclosed in order to get their way, and they are careful to resolve conflicts without resorting to criticism that does injury to the child.

- Having been told that the child is easily frightened about being separated from them in a public place, they do not threaten to abandon the reluctant boy or girl who is absorbed with a toy and doesn't want to leave the store. "All right, you can stay and play, but we are going on without you!" Now the child may regret revealing this private insecurity to parents. Better to appeal to the child's maturity by respecting his or her capacity for reason: "We need to leave now in order to be able to meet your grandparents for lunch."

- In response to an argument with what they think is right, they do not put the child's disagreement down with sarcasm in order for their opinion to prevail. "What an idea! Stupid is about as smart as you'll ever get!" Henceforth, the child may be reluctant to bring up differences for fear of getting hurt in conflict. Better to hear the child out so that he or she feels valued for speaking up: "We're glad to know your opinion, even though we're not going to change our minds."

Intimacy means risking vulnerability by allowing oneself to become deeply known. If parents want to nurture intimacy in their child, they must treat what is confided with care, and they must manage conflict in a way that encourages the child to keep speaking up when differences arise.

In addition to ensuring safety, parents can do one thing more. They can model the sharing they would like in return. They can confide to the child about their own inner lives: "Sometimes I get afraid; here is when." They can describe when they feel good about themselves and bad about themselves: "I disappointed myself today; here is how." They can describe the ups and downs of their experience at work: "I had a hard day today; here is what happened." They can allow themselves to be known on the level they would like to know their child: "I'll tell you something about me I haven't told very many people." *What they model in intimacy is ultimately what they teach.*

There are two paths to intimacy in relationships. The first is through sharing what people have *in common*, the second through sharing what they have *at difference*. In some only child families, it is the second path parents and child may find most difficult because it necessitates some degree of conflict. To ease this path, parents may want to say something like this to the child: "When we disagree, we want to treat it as an opportunity to understand more about the differences between us."

19

RISKS FROM INTIMACY

EMOTIONAL ENMESHMENT

W hat is too close for comfort? For the only child, it is when the emotional life of parents, separately or together, comes to dominate the emotional life of the boy or girl. It is when the child, to feel better himself or herself, must find a way to fix unhappiness within or between the parents. It is when the child takes responsibility for parental well-being, and faults himself or herself when unable to make things right. It is when the child's emotional state depends on the emotional state of the parents: "If they are feeling happy or unhappy, then so am I." It is at this point that intimacy can cause the child to feel trapped, to feel enmeshed with parents. Emotional independence has been lost.

- "My dad could get so discouraged and self-critical; I had to cheer him up and give him lots of praise. My job was to get him feeling good about himself when he felt bad."
- "My mom was always so guilty and easily depressed when anything went wrong; I had to give her constant reassurance that she wasn't to blame, and keep encouraging her no matter what. My job was to keep her going when she wanted to give up."
- "My parents were incompatible in so many ways—different likes and dislikes, different temperaments, always grating on each other. I was the only reason they stayed together, so it was my job to act happy to make them as happy as I could. I felt their marriage depended upon me."

Only children can be both beneficiaries and victims of intimacy with parents. To keep them from becoming victims of excessive attachment, *limits* must be set. In doing so, there are some warning signs parents can look for to discover if intimacy is enmeshing the only child in their emotional life.

- Does the child act anxious—look worried, repeatedly ask what is wrong, cling for security—when parents become upset with each other or within themselves?
- Does the child's mood seem to rise and fall with parental moods?
- Does the child try to cheer everybody up, divert attention, or attempt to figure out and fix the parental problem?
- Does the child act as mediator in parental conflicts?
- Does the child automatically implicate himself or herself in the problem by assuming he or she must have done something wrong?

If the answer to any of these questions is "yes," then parents have some important self-evaluation and explanation to do, attempting to reset limits in both cases.

In *self-evaluation*, they can ask themselves: "Are we depending on our only child to take care of us when we are suffering from emotional duress? To make us feel better? To take our mind off our problems? To distract us from tensions with each other?" If so, they need to take that responsibility back.

In *explanation*, they can declare something like this. "We appreciate how you want to take care of us when we feel unhappy with ourselves or with each other. But we want you to know that is not your job. Like everybody else, we will have our ups and downs, most of which have nothing to do with you. Our feelings are not yours to fix; they are for us to manage. When something feels wrong, we will tell you so you don't feel you are imagining. But for privacy, we may not say exactly what it is. We will, however, tell you when we have worked it out and are feeling better."

This is a lot to expect a young child to understand. Only children, however, have a maturity of understanding upon which parents can often presume. The main point is to free the child by establishing sufficient separation so that the boundaries of emotional independence and responsibility remain clear.

20

APPROVAL SEEKING

STRENGTHS FROM WANTING TO PLEASE

"Good job!" "Way to go!" "Well done!" "Congratulations!" These are common statements parents make to show approval of their child's performance. Because such expressions feel so affirming, the young child often equates parental approval with parental love: "They love me when I do well."

Although parental approval can feel like love, and parental love can amplify the power of their approval for the child, parents need to help the little boy or girl understand that this equation is false. If they do not, he or she may confuse the two and jump to some painful misunderstandings.

The chain of childish reasoning seems to run something like this:

"If I want to be loved by my parents, I must earn their approval";

"If I want to earn their approval, I must please them";

"If I want to please them, I must do well or act right";

"If I don't do well or act right, they'll be disappointed with me";

"If I disappoint them, they won't be pleased with me";

"If I don't please them, they will disapprove of me";

"If they disapprove of me, I will lose their love."

Love and Approval Are Not the Same

In general, it is helpful for parents to separate these two responses—love and approval—so the child can understand the constant nature of the first, and the transitory nature of the second. To clarify this separation, they can demonstrate by loyalty and explain in words how *love is unconditional and abiding*. It represents a *commitment* of devotion that is unwavering and will not be broken. It is a *given*. "We love you *because* you are our child, and we always will."

They can pass judgment and explain in words to show how *approval is conditional and temporary*. It represents an *evaluation* of the degree to which the child, at a given moment in time, is acting in accord with what the parents value or desire. It is *earned*. "We approve of your conduct *if and when* it pleases us." *Approval doesn't prove love any more than love guarantees approval.* The two are independent and need to be kept that way.

This separation can be hard to maintain, however, in an only child family where the son or daughter doesn't want to disappoint parents, and where parents are dedicated to doing all they can to make the child happy. Pleasing each other can feel like the best way for parents and child to keep their attachment strong.

"When I was very young, it felt like growing up in a mutual appreciation society. I wanted to do my best to please them, and they wanted to do their best to please me. That was why those early years were so happy and felt so full of love. And it worked wonderfully well, until I hit middle school. Then we began to act in ways each other didn't like—to disagree, to argue, and to fight. I complained and rebelled. They criticized and corrected. It was a hard time. None of us felt as loved as we did before."

When mutual pleasing is in effect, as so often happens during the early childhood years, an idealized relationship can become the norm. Many parents do not give up these golden years at adolescence without a sincere sense of loss, even betrayal. "You used to be such a wonderful child; what's happened to you?"

In moderation, and distinguished from loving, there is nothing wrong in parents and the only child wanting to please each other and enjoying each other's approval. In fact, *one of the delights in parenting an only child is the pure pleasure each enjoys bringing pleasure to the other*. This synergy of pleasing is a powerful one: approval that comes in response to being pleasing only increases the desire to please some more. Efforts made for the happiness of each other makes most only child families, at least until the abrasion of adolescence sets in, very satisfying and harmonious homes to live in.

The Pitfalls of Praise

Probably the most helpful way to nurture strengths from mutual pleasing is to avoid the pitfalls of excessive and indiscriminate praise. Particularly when the child is very young, pleasing parents is a powerful motivation for doing what they want. Learning to walk, becoming toilet trained, starting to pick up after himself or herself are effectively encouraged with massive doses of praise. "Wow!" thinks the child, "I really pleased my parents this time!" *Parental praise provides extrinsic motivation.*

As the child grows older, however, parents need to measure out their praise to preserve its worth. Praise automatically given for any act of performance becomes routine, cheapening its value from frequency of use. "My parents think everything I do is great." *Better to keep praise selective.* As mentioned before when discussing power of attention, what parents tell the child about how he or she is determines much about how the child comes to see himself or herself.

During the preschool years, the only child is likely to consider whatever parents say as true. Therefore, by enthusiastically praising the boy's or girl's ordinary efforts as exceptional, parents may convince the child of superiority to others. In consequence, the boy or girl may feel encouraged to act socially condescending to peers. By keeping praise in proportion to accomplishment, parents can help prevent the child's self-expectations from becoming grandiose. *Better to keep praise realistic.*

In the family, praise is a form of approval that provides the child with feedback about having pleased the powers that be, the parents. General praise tends to be affirming, but is otherwise uninformative: "We think you're wonderful!" What has the child learned about how to estimate his or her capacity? *Better to keep praise specific:* "You have a talent for arranging things to look pretty, which comes out when you set the table."

Extreme praise, by creating high expectations, can create pressure. Thinks the child: "If my parents think I'm some kind of a genius, I'd better excel in whatever I do." *Better to keep praise moderate.*

To nurture strengths from pleasing, parents can mix expressions of pleasure at the *process* of relationship with the child ("I had such fun being with you at the park today!") with expression of pleasure with the child's *performance* ("You played a good game today!"). Although not always true, men, because they were often socialized to draw esteem from quality of performance growing up, tend to express more approval in response to how the child is *doing.* Women, on the other hand, because they were often socialized to draw esteem from quality of relationships growing up, tend to express more approval to how the child is *being.* When both ways of pleasing are given value by each parent, praise for each encourages the child to preserve the mix: "I am valued both for how I am and how I do."

21

~~~~~~

RISKS FROM APPROVAL SEEKING

THE TYRANNY OF PLEASING

P arents and the only child frequently have a very low tolerance for displeasing each other. The emotional costs of offending, hurting, or letting the other down can be extremely hard to bear. "I feel like a bad parent to my child." "I feel like a disappointment to my parents." Both want to protect the other from injury, and in the process protect themselves: "When I make you unhappy, I feel just miserable myself."

When a mutual *tyranny of pleasing* becomes established, parents and the only child can pay a price. Striving to avoid parental disapproval, the child may sacrifice authenticity in order to please. Striving to avoid disapproval from their son or daughter, parents may be unwilling to set healthy limits that displease the child.

On the child's side, he or she may be tyrannized by the question: "Am I doing well enough to satisfy my parents?" The boy or girl may be reluctant to disappoint a parental expectation no matter how unrealistic it may be: "I can't let my parents know they are demanding too much." So he or she commits to a level of performance that entails significant stress, instead of declaring: "I know you don't like my refusing to take all honor's classes, but with everything else I am doing, that is too much pressure for me to handle."

On the parents' side, they may be tyrannized by the question: "Are we doing all we can to make our child happy?" They may be reluctant to risk unpopularity by refusing their only child's excessive or inappropriate requests: "We just can't say 'no.'" So they put their son or daughter at risk of more freedom than is good for the child, instead of declaring: "We know you don't like our not letting you go, but the situation is too unsupervised to be safe."

In addition to clearly separating love from approval, to encouraging the child to speak up even at the cost of displeasing parents, and to speaking up themselves at the cost of displeasing the child, there are some statements parents might want to consider avoiding that tend to make the tyranny of pleasing worse. These are *crushing statements* that can threaten a significant loss of worth in the parents' eyes.

- *"We're proud of you"* suggests a linkage between how well the child does and how good parents feel about themselves. In service of this connection, the child can become burdened by the belief that his or her performance is a major pillar of parental self-esteem. Do badly, and parents may feel badly about themselves. Better for them to say: "Good for you!" "Good going!" "We're happy for you!"

- *"We're disappointed in you"* suggests that the child has lost loving standing in parental esteem. Most only children cannot emotionally afford such a loss. Better to say: "We need to help you find a way to do better next time."

- *"You really let us down"* suggests the weight of parental dependency that the only child must support, responsible for their well-being as well as his or her own. Better to say: "We were expecting something else."

- *"How could you do this to us?"* suggests that the child's mistakes or misconduct had malicious intent. Because most only children are inclined to feel guilty when they inadvertently hurt their parents, they are unlikely to do so deliberately. Better to say: "We need to talk with you about what happened so it does not happen again."

- *"Why can't you behave as well as they do?"* suggests that by comparison parents prefer other children to their own. Most only children are emotionally unprepared to compete for parental approval with other children. Better to say: "We would like you to act differently; here is how."
- *"You never do anything right!"* suggests blanket condemnation with no hope for redemption. An only child needs to know that no specific bad act can ever violate parental faith in the child's capacity for good. Better to say: "You did it wrong this time; let's figure out a way for you to get it right next time."
- *"We give up on you!"* suggests that parents have lost their capacity to keep on caring how the child does or does not do. Abandonment of love, the only child's worst fear, is actualized by such a declaration. Better to say: "We intend to hang in there and help you get this problem straightened out."

As in helping, so in parenting, the first injunction is to try to do no harm. Thus, parents do not want to say things that only make the tyranny of pleasing any worse for the only child than it already may be.

In addition, parents may want to repeat the following statement to themselves until they can begin to believe it: *"Acting badly does not mean our child is bad or that we are bad parents. Good parents have good children who will sometimes make bad decisions in the normal trial and error process of growing up."*

By accepting the inevitability of some misbehavior in their child, and by the child accepting parental correction as a normal consequence when these incidents occur, parents and the only child can reduce the tyranny of pleasing in their relationship. It is unrealistic for either party to expect perfection either from themselves or from the other.

22

EXPECTATIONS

STRENGTHS FROM BEING REALISTIC

This is one of the longest Keys in this book for a reason. It provides a *model for managing expectations* that can help parents avoid much unnecessary conflict from misunderstanding their only child.

Because most parents of only children are first-time parents, they have no previous child-rearing experience upon which to base reasonable expectations for their child or for themselves. Consequently, one of the major challenges of parenting an only child is establishing expectations that accurately fit the reality of their growing child and their role as the child changes.

Three Kinds of Expectations

Expectations are mental sets that people create to anticipate what is going to happen to their life as they move through *time* (from present to future) and through major *change* (from old to new). Becoming parents is just such a change. "What is our child going to be like?" wonder the parents. "What is parenting going to be like?" They don't know.

Rather than allow the unknown to keep them totally unprepared, however, they answer these questions by formulating *three categories of expectations* to increase their sense of confidence with foresight and to reduce their fear from ignorance with information:

1. They may make *predictions:* about what the child's physical state *will* be, for example. "Our child *will* be healthy."
2. They may have *ambitions:* about how they *want* the child to behave, for example. "We *want* our child to be cuddly and responsive."
3. They may set *conditions:* about on how the child *should* fit into their busy lives, for example. "Within a month, our child *should* be sleeping soundly through the night."

If their expectations for the child fit the reality they encounter, they experience a positive emotional outcome. When their *prediction* of wellness is met, they feel *secure.* When their *ambition* of loving closeness is met, they feel *fulfilled.* When their *condition* of accommodation to their life is met, they feel *satisfied.* Expectations on target, the parents feel content with their lot as a new family: "This is exactly how we imagined having a child would be."

When Expectations Are Violated

Suppose, however, expectations of their only child are frustrated instead. Perhaps the infant becomes afflicted with persistent bouts of colic. When they try to give the screaming child comfort, sometimes he or she becomes more fussy and rejects their loving touch. At four months old, the child is still waking them up at night crying from distress. Now their initial expectations have been violated: "This is not how we thought parenting would be!" In consequence, a different set of emotional outcomes occur.

- Because their *prediction* of wellness is violated, parents can feel *surprised* and may sometimes become *anxious:* "Will we ever figure out what to do to make her feel better?"
- Because their *ambition* for affection is violated, parents can feel *disappointed* and may sometimes become *sad:* "I want to be able to hold and comfort him, and I can't."

- Because their *condition* for accommodation to the adult schedule is violated, parents can feel *betrayed* and may sometimes become *angry:* "Just once that kid should let us get a good night's sleep!"

Adjusting Expectations

Now the parents have two problems, not just one. They have the problem of a child mysteriously afflicted with colic, and they have the violated expectations that they are feeling. Even with medical consultation about foods and feeding strategies, there may not be much they can do about the first problem, but they can certainly alleviate the second.

Expectations are not genetic or fixed. They are chosen and can be flexible. For parents to hold on to unrealistic expectations in the face of a reality they cannot change is to set themselves up for emotional distress—for anxiety, sadness, and anger. Better for them to adjust their expectations to fit the existing reality of their child.

- "Our child *will* continue to be bothered by this complaint until we find some cure or he outgrows it."
- "Although we *want* to physically comfort our child, we know sometimes it only makes her more fussy."
- "We *should* expect to have interrupted sleep as long as the child's pain continues."

Managing to Keep Expectations in the Family Realistic

Because parents want to do so well by their only child, and often want their only child to do so well by them, it is very easy for their expectations of the child and of themselves to become unrealistic. When violations ensue, an emotional price is usually paid. Because relationships in an only child family are so sensitively close, and violations can be so strongly felt, the realistic management of expectations becomes critical to everyone's well-being.

Strengths from sharing and clarifying expectations include enabling family members *to anticipate change* (preparing for the new and different), *to coordinate their efforts* (making workable arrangements and agreements), and *to communicate their needs* in relationship (discussing what they would like from each other). In all these ways and more, talking about expectations can keep them well connected.

Expectations and Change

Consider a young couple entering first-time parenthood, and how this transition can be eased when they clarify with each other the three kinds of expectations.

- "We *will* have more expenses, so let's talk about how to save and spend our money when we have a child." (They talk about *predictions*.)
- "We still *want* to have enough separate time for the marriage, so let's talk about how to preserve some time alone together." (They talk about *ambitions*.)
- "We *should* be willing to give up some personal freedom for the sake of our child, so let's talk about how to share this new responsibility." (They talk about *conditions*.)

Setting joint expectations in anticipation of a new and different experience can reduce the likelihood of surprise, disappointment, and betrayal when the change arrives.

Expectations and Coordination

One major strength of sharing expectations is the sense of understanding and agreement that helps all parties in a relationship feel like they are "working from the same page." Parenthood is a partnership that requires cooperation. Without clarification of expectations, however, even the most willing cooperation can result in miscommunication. "I thought you were going to stay home tonight with the baby so I could go out with friends!" protests parent number one when parent number two, claiming ignorance, objects to this plan. "You just *assumed* I would, you mean," replies the angry other who had been expecting family time together. "Don't automatically expect me to do what we haven't actually discussed." *The road to much marital conflict is paved with false assumptions.*

Expectations and Communication

Just as clarifying expectations allows parents to follow a mutually understood and agreed upon course of action with each other, so clarifying their expectations of the only child is important to avoid unnecessary misunderstanding and conflict.

Thus, at the beginning of the third grade, for example, when their only child moves up to a more demanding level of work and responsibility at school, parents can clarify some of their expectations.

- "This is one thing we assume you *will* do—come home directly after school." (*Predictions* are the basis for creating *plans*.)
- "This is one thing we *want* you to do—maintain a B average." (*Ambitions* are the basis for setting *goals*.)
- "This is one thing we believe you absolutely *should* do—your homework." (*Conditions* are the basis for making *stipulations*.)

As parents clarify their expectations—their plans, their goals, their stipulations—for the only child, the boy or girl comes to know where they stand. The child who can honestly say "I know what my parents expect of me," usually feels well connected (although not always in agreement) with family.

Critical Family Situations in Which to Clarify Expectations

Routine communication about what they believe will happen, what they want to have happen, and what they believe should happen is what allows parents and the only child to remain on the same course with each other. There are, however, particular situations where parents need to be sure that expectations are clarified with their only child.

- Anytime a major change is going to occur for the family (such as a parent taking a new job that entails a significant alteration in schedule), it is important to clarify what routine will be the same and what may change for the child.
- Anytime a member of the family feels subject to inappropriate or unrealistic expectations (such as feeling like he or she is being asked to do too much), that person must speak up and try to get the expectations more reasonably set.
- Anytime one member knows he or she is going to violate another's expectation (such as getting home later than promised), the violator needs to commit to correcting that expectation as soon as possible.
- Anytime one member doesn't know what to expect from another and starts imagining the worst (such as interpreting the other person's silence as disappointment or anger), he or she needs to commit to ask for clarification about what is actually going on.
- Anytime there is going to be a significant separation between parents and the only child (such as the child going away to an overnight summer camp), they need to set expectations about the manner and frequency of communication while they are apart.

Expectations are communication linkages that continually keep everybody clear about what is happening and what is going to happen, keeping family members feeling close because they stay adequately and realistically informed.

23

~~~~~~

RISKS FROM EXPECTATIONS

TRANSITION AND CORRECTION

There are two common experiences that can create turmoil in the only child family because, in each case, the risk of violated expectations is very high. *Major transitions* in the child's growth is the first, and how parents manage *corrective discipline* with the child is the second.

Managing Transitions

Transitions take a person from an old to a new reality. An example of a major transition for the child would include the entry into elementary school. For parents, an example would be adjusting to the onset of their child's adolescence. Unrealistic expectations about each change can make each transition significantly more difficult.

The Child's Expectations About School

From being the sole focus of adult attention and estimating self-worth through the parents' loving eyes, the only child may develop some unrealistic expectations about life at school. Parents can elicit these expectations in advance by asking the little boy or girl: "What *will* school be like; what do you *want* it to be like; how do you believe it *should* work?" In response, the child may declare a prediction, ambition, and condition about this new experience that may *not* fit the reality of school.

- The child's prediction might be: "I *will* be given choices about whatever I'm asked to do."
- The child's ambition might be: "I always *want* to be praised for what I do."
- The child's condition might be: "I *should* be allowed all the time I need to get my work done."

To the degree that these expectations prove unrealistic, the child may experience significant emotional distress. Acting fearful, sad, or angry in class, he or she may provoke a negative response from the teacher who is determined to treat the only child as just one student among many.

Parents can help the child avoid unnecessary emotional upset by resetting expectations that more accurately fit the new situation.

- "Unlike at home where we give you lots of choices, at school you will be told what to do."
- "Unlike at home where we always appreciate what you do, at school the teacher won't praise you so often because there are so many other children wanting attention."
- "Unlike at home where we allow whatever time you need to get your work done, at school you must finish your work within the schedule the teacher sets."

Parental Expectations About Adolescence

Because parents often have such an idyllic relationship with their only child, they are often unprepared for the normal tensions and strains that adolescence can bring (see Part Eight, beginning on page 127). Then, in a state of violated expectations, they can allow their own anxiety, sadness, or anger at differences they did not anticipate to govern their response to this new phase in their child's growth.

Parents who anticipate that adolescence is not going to change their old relationship with the child, may be entering a major transition with unrealistic expectations.

- "We assume that our teenager *will* be as open and communicative as ever." (Their prediction.)
- "We assume that our teenager *wants* to spend as much time with us as ever." (Their ambition.)
- "We assume that our teenager *should* be as helpful and compliant as ever." (Their condition.)

When these expectations do not fit the changes that adolescence has created, they can feel surprised, disappointed, or betrayed. Realistic expectations about the change would have served them better.

- "We assume that our teenager *will* be somewhat less communicative than before in order to create more privacy from us";
- "We assume that our teenager will *want* to spend more time with friends and socialize somewhat less with us";
- "We assume that our teenager *should* be somewhat more resistant about meeting our household requests."

Just as it benefits the only child to enter school with realistic expectations, so it benefits parents of an only child to have realistic expectations about the normal changes adolescence brings.

Managing Correction

Violating parental expectations through mistakes or misbehavior can cause the child to worry about having damaged his or her relationship to the parents in the process. In fact, the boy or girl may have grounds for this concern based on how the mother and father react. The parents may act surprised ("We feel frightened because you didn't keep us adequately informed"), may act disappointed ("We feel let down that you failed to do as you agreed"), or may act betrayed ("We feel angry that you broke one of our rules").

The challenge for parents is to show the child that just because their disapproval has been earned, their love has not been lost. How they manage to communicate their expectations is the key to effectively meeting this challenge of communicating acceptance while giving disciplinary correction.

Two Sets of Expectations

Parents have *two sets of expectations* to manage when addressing their only child's misbehavior: expectations of acceptance and expectations for change. *Expectations of acceptance* reduce pressure on the child: "No matter how you act, we love who and how you are." Expectations of acceptance communicate *unconditional love* and are for *connecting*. The prediction states: "We will always love you." The ambition states: "We want you to be how you are." The condition states: "We should always be there for you to count on." The only child who feels that these parental expectations are firmly in place is best able to withstand the impact of the second set of parental expectations (of change) when they become necessary to express.

Expectations for change increase pressure on the child: "When you are not living within our demands and limits, we shall take issue with your conduct." Expectations for change communicate *responsible caring* and are for *correcting*. The prediction states: "We will speak up for your best interests against what you may like to hear." The ambition states: "We want you to act in ways that serve you well, not badly." The condition states: "As your parents, we should provide a source of direction in your life and we intend to do just that." The only child who feels these expectations are in place knows he or she is growing up in a strong family structure under close supervision.

Acceptance Before and After Correction

Understanding the distinction between the two sets of expectations, parents can assert discipline in such a way that the only child feels secure in their love when being subjected to their disciplinary disapproval. Before demanding correction, they first confirm connection so the child does not fear rejection: "They are through with me for how I have acted." Therefore, parents first state their expectations of acceptance: "How you have acted in no way affects our love for you." After affirming this basic connection, parents then state their expectations of change: "How you have acted must be corrected and consequences must be faced." And finally, after correction and reparation have been made, parents then *normalize* the relationship by restating their expectations of acceptance: "Let's get on with living together as we always have."

Normalization can be accomplished by parents reasserting their unconditional commitment of acceptance.

- "We think well of you as always" (as opposed to a statement of rejection: "We're still disappointed in you").
- "We have faith in you as always" (as opposed to a statement of rejection: "We just give up on you").
- "We love you as always" (as opposed to a statement of rejection: "We don't care what you do anymore").

24

^^

AMBITION

STRENGTHS FROM WANTING TO DO WELL

Of the three categories of expectations—predictions, ambitions, and conditions—*ambitions* is the one that probably complicates the parent/only child relationship the most. Ambitions raise two troubling questions:

1. What standards and goals do parents want their child to achieve?
2. How well must the child perform to feel he or she is doing well enough?

At the heart of these questions is the relationship between *investment* and *return*. Parents invest more hope, time, energy, and resources in an only child than they do in multiple children individually because they do not have to divide what they have to give. As for the notion of a return, parenting is not a purely altruistic endeavor. It is also partly selfish. With any number of children, parents expect something back for all their love and effort and sacrifice. From an only child, however, they expect the most return of all because he or she is the only source of child satisfaction they have.

The boy's or girl's performance is one part of parental satisfaction, often taken as a measure of all the conscientious parenting they give: "How well our child performs shows how successful our parenting is." Most parents are ambitious for their only child. They want to do well by this son or daughter and they want him or her to do well by them. "We only want the best *for* you" can be a coded message for "We only want the best *from* you."

Aware of the enormous investment parents have made in his or her life, the only child (sometimes feeling grateful, or obligated, or even guilty) often wants to make a commensurate return. "My parents have done so much for me. Whatever I wanted they supported if they possibly could. They've been behind me 100 percent, so I've tried to give them back something to be proud of." *Only children tend to be ambitious for themselves partly for the sake of their parents.*

Equal Standing

Growing up in a nuclear family of adults, the only child soon learns to put himself or herself on an equal social standing with parents. Identifying with and imitating their ways, the boy or girl comes to feel more their social equal than their inferior. Give and take comes naturally. Speaking up, expressing opinions, and expecting to be consulted about family decisions all feel like a birthright. Not intimidated by parental authority, the only child is often not intimidated by external authority as well. Parental friends, with whom the child learns to socialize, usually consider him or her socially precocious, impressed by adult-like manners and skills in one so young. "How grown-up you are!" is a common compliment they give.

Rewarded for seeming older than his or her years, the only child usually rises to meet these expectations by learning to act more and more socially mature. "Of course I knew I was a child, but I also knew that I was supposed to act grown-up. My parents didn't want to baby me because they didn't want to keep me acting like a baby. They wanted me to join their world as soon as I could. They treated me as a little adult, and so did I. They didn't pull rank on me. They explained what they wanted from me and why. Even though they made the rules, I was their equal as a person."

Equal Standards

In consequence of being "adultized" from assuming equal standing, the only child, usually unbeknownst to parents, then makes a very formative resolve: "Since I consider myself to be their social equal, then I want to be as capable as they are too." *The child goes from assuming equal standing with parents to wanting to apply equal (adult) standards for his or her own performance.*

Without the urging of parents, the only child usually internalizes a very high set of personal ambitions that are derived from the social equivalence he or she feels with them. For this reason, parents of only children usually need *not,* and probably should not, push or pressure their son or daughter to achieve. There is already enough built-in motivation to suffice.

Keeping Pressure Down

Because the only child is usually so highly motivated (a disproportionate number of medical doctors, for example, are first or only children), the parental job is not so much to mobilize as to humanize this ambition. This means helping the child keep performance expectations realistic and humane. In doing so, parents can speak to a number of issues that can encourage the child to keep personal performance pressure down.

- When the girl or boy gets upset at not being able to do a task as easily or as well as parents, the parents may want to gently remind the child that she or he is not yet an adult. They have had more years to practice what the child is now learning to do for the first time. "Don't measure yourself against us. That's not being fair to you."

- When the girl or boy shows signs of treating performance as the only pillar of self-esteem that matters ("I'm only as worthwhile as my accomplishments"), parents may want to remind the child that she or he is a human being first, and a human doer second. "Our love for you, and we hope your love for yourself, is based not on what you achieve, but simply on who you are."

- When the girl or boy is crestfallen from failing to meet a personal ambition, parents may want to remind the child that, in the long run, effort is more important than outcome, and that there is no failure except failure to try. "You always learn something from trying, and every effort you make only strengthens your capacity to work hard for whatever else you want to achieve."

Sometimes a highly motivated only child can be unduly hard upon himself or herself. To nurture ambition, parents can encourage the child to refrain from self-punishment. They can also help the child from becoming unduly self-critical by modeling a lack of undue self-criticism themselves.

25

RISKS FROM AMBITION
UNMET DREAMS AND PERFECTIONISM

There are traps set for parents and only children around the issue of ambition.

The parent traps are:

- needing to compensate through the boy or girl for childhood deprivation of their own;
- and needing to fulfill dreams through the child for themselves.

The child traps are:

- needing to fulfill the unmet aspirations of parents through his or her own achievement;
- and needing to perform so highly that anything less than perfection feels like relative failure.

Parents Who Need Compensation

Those parents with strong achievement agendas of their own can confuse ambitions for themselves with ambitions for their child. Suppose, for example, an adult grew up in a family in which adversity severely limited the amount of time, nurturance, and material resources parents could devote to their children. Overcoming childhood deprivation with determination, this adult resolves to compensate for what was missed when it comes time to have a family. "I want my child to have it better than I did. I want to be able to give what my parents couldn't give to me."

Driven by this personal ambition, the parent treats the child as a chance to revise the course of history, creating in the present what was lacking in the past. When the child, however, is not receptive, appreciative, or responsive to this ambition, parents can feel disappointed to a degree that bewilders the child. "I never understood why my mom praised me for every little thing and then got angry because I took her praise for granted." (Because the mom grew up in a family where no praise was given.) "I never understood why my dad wanted to be so involved in my sports, and felt so hurt when I didn't want him for my coach." (Because the dad grew up in a family where no parental involvement was given.) *When parents give to their only child what they wished they had received themselves, pressure on the boy or girl to provide a satisfying return can feel extreme, as well as disappointment when he or she does not.*

Parents who have suffered deprivation growing up need to heal themselves from whatever hurts they carry into adulthood without depending on their only child to be a source of salvation. If they know their own unfinished business from growing up is causing them to overinvest in or overreact to their child, they may want to get counseling help to work on their own recovery.

Fulfilling Personal Dreams

Dream connections are another area of vulnerability for parents. Two kinds of dreams can amplify the power of their ambitions: dreams of similarity and dreams of differentness. A *similarity dream* might be: "I wanted my child to be socially involved and have a large circle of friends like I did; but she prefers to spend her time alone instead." Parental disappointment in the girl's solitary path through school may encourage the daughter to feel disappointed in herself: "I'll never be as popular as Mom was or as she wants me to be." A *differentness dream* might be: "I wanted my son to graduate high school and not drop out to work like I did, but that is just what he has done." Parental disappointment at the boy's educational choice may encourage the son to feel disappointed in himself: "I'll never be the student Dad wanted." *Parents need to be sensitive to ambitions that are connected to their dreams, because, when violated, their disappointment can have a crushing impact on their only child.*

It can be helpful for parents to take an inventory of their own *dream agendas*. This can easily be done by asking themselves two questions:

1. "In what ways do we feel it is very important for our child to make the *same* choices as we did growing up?"
2. "In what ways do we it feel it is very important for our child to make *different* choices than we did growing up?"

The answers can represent emotionally loaded areas of concern for parents. Knowing these concerns in advance helps keep parents from overreacting when dream ambitions are violated by the child. Also helpful is remembering that what was of value for the parents may not be of value to the child, and what may have been a mistake for the parents may not be a mistake for the child.

The Child Who Wants to Fulfill Parental Dreams

For the only child, the trap of striving to fulfill unmet parental aspirations is sprung by a sense of obligation to accomplish what they were not able to accomplish for themselves. A daughter may confide: "My mom sacrificed her own desire for a college education by working and saving so I could get mine. That's partly why I went to college instead of starting a full-time job. This degree is not just for me, it's at least as much for her." Or a son may confide: "No matter how hard he tried, my dad never did well in business. It was always hand-to-mouth. So I wanted to make a lot of money in business not just for myself, but for him to enjoy a sense of financial success through me." *Only children can get caught up in devoting their lives to satisfying the unmet aspirations of their parents.*

To prevent this servitude from developing, parents can make sure they are not pushing the child to satisfy their longings, and they can also make a statement to free the child. "Just as we have made decisions in life to meet our needs and not live out the lives of our parents, we want you to make choices in life because they work for you, not out of some duty to us."

The Child Who Wants to Be Perfect

Another entrapping ambition is wanting to be perfect for parents. "When your parents think you are perfect, say you are perfect, and treat you as perfect, that's how you try to be. Anything less would disappoint them, and who would want to do that? If there is one thing I have never wanted to be guilty of, it is letting my parents down!"

When all parental aspirations are centered on a single child, the pressure from that ambition can cause the boy or girl to try to do everything right, to be as successful as parents want, to demonstrate that he or she is after all, and first of all, the exceptional child they wanted. To strive to fulfill this unrealistic ideal, the only child must endure the twin pressures that perfectionism creates: to live error-free (to avoid making mistakes at all costs), and to always excel (and not fail at all costs).

Ideals like perfection are double-edged: they can ennoble and inspire, but they can also dehumanize and discourage. Being ideal is not real. Being ideal is not human because "to err is human." The only child, however, may not see such idealism for what it is—unreality.

A Sense of Relative Failure

One common legacy of only childhood is a sense of relative failure and even a sense of fraud. No matter how hard the child strives, when internalized ideals cannot be met, a troubling feeling of inadequacy is often the result. "I never measured up to what was expected of me, or at least what I expected of myself. It's taken me a long time to accept that being average is okay. But every time I see my parents, they treat me like they always have—like some kind of extremely accomplished person whom they admire. I always come away feeling mixed. It feels good to be so well thought of, and bad to know I'm not really as wonderful and successful as they want to believe I am."

For many only children, this sense of disappointment persists as long as the grown man or woman believes he or she has not lived up to the lofty ambitions of parents, and of himself or herself.

A Sense of Futility About Achievement

Contributing to this feeling of disappointment can be a streak of underachievement when standards of perfection are used to justify giving up: "If I can't do it perfectly, then I'd rather not do it at all." Or the other extreme can be a streak of overachievement, creating constant stress from striving to live up to ideals: "Even if I succeed in doing things well today, I still have to worry about doing everything right tomorrow." *The demands of perfection can discourage the only child from trying, or impel the only child to strive unmercifully hard.*

Parents can try to moderate the risks of perfection in a number of helpful ways.

- When the girl or boy is striving for an unrealistic objective, parents may want to remind the child of a third alternative. "Goals are for guiding your efforts. Standards are for giving you a rough measure to work by. Neither is meant to be used to cause you stress and suffering. Instead of beating up on yourself for failing to do as well as you initially wanted, we hope you can appreciate what you were able to accomplish."

- When the girl or boy is reluctant to try something new because she or he cannot do it well right away or at all, or refuses to participate because of fearing she or he cannot compete to win, parents may want to remind the child that personal growth is more important than the level of achievement. Trying oneself out in new and different ways when young is how a child develops a healthy variety of capacities to carry on to adulthood. "If you limit what you do to only what you comfortably do well, then you will miss out learning a lot of skills that are important when it comes time to take care of yourself later on."

- When the girl or boy shows signs of feeling like a relative failure, depreciating herself or himself for not measuring up to some personal ideal of achievement, parents might want to tell the child that she or he is responsible for creating the set of expectations within which one can feel either bad or good. Then they can describe *expectations of rejection* and *expectations of acceptance*. Expectations of rejection say: "I *will* never measure up, I *want* to do better than I have, I *should* never be satisfied with myself." Expectations of acceptance say: "I *will* do what I can, I *want* to enjoy what I accomplish, I *should* esteem myself for who and how I am." An only child who is personally committed to expectations of acceptance is not likely to consider himself or herself a relative failure or to experience a sense of fraud. *To a large degree, the quality of his or her inner personal life is dependent on the self-accepting or self-rejecting nature of expectations that the only child holds.*

26

~~~~~~

RESPONSIBILITY

STRENGTHS FROM INDEPENDENCE

"Be responsible" is an implicit message the only child tends to receive as part of identifying with the adult status of parents as he or she strives to act socially mature from an early age.

A heightened sense of responsibility just seems to come with the territory of being an only child. "To me, being responsible meant acting grown-up just like my parents. Doing the kinds of things for myself they did for themselves. Simple things. Cleaning up after myself. Keeping promises to them like they kept promises to me. Finishing what I started. Giving help where I could. That's how my parents were, so that's how I tried to be."

For many only children, having parents as sole companions in the family encourages acquiring a lot of behaviors often identified with being responsible:

- being self-regulated (observing a schedule without reminders),
- picking up after oneself (putting back what is taken out),
- making up one's own mind (solving problems for oneself),
- acting independently (not waiting to be told what to do),
- accepting consequences (owning the outcome of personal choice),
- following rules (being socially obedient),

- keeping commitments (honoring one's word),
- doing one's work (completing what has been assigned),
- being honest (speaking the truth about feelings and actions).

Many only children tend to have a head start when it comes to learning the various forms of responsibility.

Parents can build on the early base of responsibility in their only child by thinking ahead. They can ask themselves two very powerful questions about the child's future:

1. "Is there anything that we are doing for our child at this point that she could be learning to do independently?" If so, they can begin transferring responsibility for accomplishing some of those tasks now. Thus, the young child can begin assuming simple basics of self-care when parents believe they have given adequate instruction and practice to safely let them go. The young child can learn to bathe himself, pick out his clothes, and make lunch for school. One dividend of transferring responsibility is increasing the child's sense of competence and self-esteem. "See what I can do for myself!"
2. "By the time the adolescent leaves our care for independence, what *qualities* (honesty, for example), *skills* (the ability to earn and budget money, for example), and *experiences* (having traveled alone, for example), do we want this young person to have to be as well prepared for adult responsibility as possible?" Then they make a list of *exit responsibilities* necessary for a successful transition, and schedule at what age instruction in each responsibility should begin.

Thus, rather than simply buying their sixteen year old a secondhand car to drive, parents treat this event as a chance to teach her some important exit responsibilities: getting a job to earn and save the money, researching as a consumer, shopping for comparison, pricing insurance, estimating operating costs, budgeting to meet future expenses, and so forth.

The old advice is relevant here: It is more empowering to teach someone how to catch a fish than to simply give that person a fish to eat. It better serves the growth of responsibility for a young person to earn and learn how to buy a car than to simply receive one without making any effort, without acquiring any understanding, or without developing any worldly skills. This kind of involvement in the process of major life decision making is costly both in terms of parental labor and time. However, parents of an only child are usually in an extremely strong position to afford both expenses.

How Responsibility Is Learned

Teaching responsibility is a matter of supervised preparation and timed release from parental control, at which point the child:

- *assumes freedom of choice* in some area of his or her life (walking to school as rehearsed with the parent many times before, for example),
- *puts his or her well-being at risk* of personal decision making (must make five turns and cross three busy streets),
- *owns the consequences* of those choices (admits that he or she made a wrong turn somewhere and is lost),
- and *recovers from those consequences* (asks directions and finally finds the right way).

A child's growth from dependence to independence is only possible if there is a gathering of responsibility over time. A central dilemma of parenting is when to let go of control and give more freedom in order to create the opportunity for responsibility to be learned. On one extreme, parents know that giving total freedom (utter permissiveness) is no protection, so they must hold on to some control. On the other extreme, parents know that total control (complete protection) is no preparation, so they must let go and allow some freedom of experience and choice.

How do parents strengthen the only child's power of responsibility? By letting go of degrees of choice as soon as they reasonably can, using existing evidence of responsibility and exit goals for responsibility as their guides. *For parents, the goal of transferring responsibility is to work themselves out of a job.*

27

RISKS FROM RESPONSIBILITY

ASSUMING TOO MUCH OWNERSHIP

One way to think about a child's growth is as a gathering of responsibility from a state of dependence (the infant totally reliant on parental care) to a state of independence (the young adult able to assume full self-support). For the parent and the only child, who are so closely wed to their relationship, the hard question about the child assuming more individual responsibility is this: To what degree does each party really want independence of each other?

When a parent gives over some freedom of control by transferring responsibility to the child, both parties suffer some loss. Each gives up some of the old connection with each other. The disconnection that is created is what contributes to the growing independence between them. The parent gives up some control to decide what the child can or cannot do. The child gives up some structural support that was provided by the parent being willing to make choices for the boy or girl.

Thus, giving the sixteen year old responsibility to drive a car creates a significant measure of independence between them because he or she no longer depends on parents to get chauffeured around. Giving this same child permission to make money at a part-time job also creates more independence, the child now depending less on parents to finance what he or she wants to buy. *The more the child learns to be self-responsible, the less involved in the child's life parents become, the less relevant and valued they may feel.*

For parents, risks of responsibility come from two sources: from wanting to do too much for their only child, and from wanting to fault their parenting when the child gets hurt or gets in trouble.

Pitfalls for Parents: Doing Too Much for the Child

Typically, the more children parents have, the less they end up doing for each child, the more they expect each one to do without or to do independently. With an only child, however, parents tend to indulge themselves by indulging the girl or boy. Each act of doing and caring for is an act of love they love to give and which the child loves to receive.

Thus an only child may confess: "I guess if I was spoiled, it wasn't from how much my parents gave me, but how much they did for me. It caused me to expect others to want to do the same, and feel disappointed when they didn't. You'd think I would have been grateful for everything my parents did for me, and in a way I was, but in a way I wasn't. Because the more they did, the more I expected them to do, the less I learned to do for myself, the less I appreciated all they did. It may sound silly, but if you're used to your parents fixing your car and doing your laundry, then it's hard to do those things for yourself when you finally leave home. Sometimes I think they felt really hurt by my response. I kept complaining that they never did enough!"

To reduce this risk of doing too much for their only child, there are three helpful questions parents can ask:

1. "What significant *activities* are we doing for the child that he or she can begin doing for himself or herself?" (Making his bed or doing her laundry, for example.)

2. "What significant *experiences* are we managing for the child that he or she could begin to learn to handle by himself or herself?" (Deciding how to spend her earnings or deciding whether to save his gift money, for example.)
3. "What significant *knowledge* are we keeping from the child that he or she could begin to understand?" (Telling him about safe sex or advising her about moderate drinking, for example.)

The hard loving of parenting an only child is getting and letting the boy or girl to gather sufficient power of responsibility over activities, experiences, and knowledge to successfully prepare for independence.

Pitfalls for Parents: Holding Themselves Too Accountable

One of the hardest limits for parents of an only child to set is the limit of their responsibility when their child gets hurt or gets in trouble. There are often two automatic questions they will ask themselves: "To what degree was this our fault?" "What could we have done differently so this would not have happened?" The temptation is to extend their responsibility into the only child's life wherever adversity strikes or misadventure occurs.

So their fifth-grader who, in the company of rebellious peers, wrote angry graffiti on the side of their elementary school is delivered home by a patrol officer. About to confess the deed, the child is interrupted by the parents: "What have we done wrong that you should do such a thing?" Ever alert to escaping full responsibility for the misdeed, for which some punishment is due, the child readily agrees. "You never said writing a few words was such a big deal! How was I to know? It's your fault for not telling me!" For parents to accept this blame is to excuse the errant child from responsibility.

To reduce their exposure to assuming excessive responsibility for misfortune that befalls their only child, parents need to *limit liability*. They can do this by accepting that there are three variables affecting their child's life that they do not control.

Limiting Parental Liability

1. *They do not control the temperament and personality of their child.* Thus, if the child is impulsive, experimental, and drawn to taking risks, they cannot change the daring nature of the boy or girl. They can only help the child learn to live with these inborn tendencies in a safe and mindful way.

2. *They do not control external circumstances in the larger world to which the child will inevitably be exposed.* Thus, most of the risks from chance encounters at school, in the community, and out in the larger world each day can neither be foreseen nor forestalled. The air is filled with germs, the streets are filled with traffic, for example. Infections are caught. Accidents do happen.

3. *They do not control the personal choices their only child makes.* Thus, despite all the instruction, supervision, and training they give, the child is ultimately governed not by parental will but by his or her own decisions. Temptation, immaturity, and ignorance all conspire to cause most only children, no matter how well parented, to get into some hurt or trouble in the course of growing up. Limited in the amount of influence they can exercise, parents are not responsible when their beloved child, who knows better, acts for the worst and in consequence must pay some hard costs.

Much of the only child's risks from responsibility come from two sources: from so identifying with adult responsibility that some actual sense of childhood is lost, and from the child taking too much responsibility for parental unhappiness.

Pitfalls for the Child: Overidentifying with Adult Responsibility

It is a very common observation made by many an only child about himself or herself, and by those adults who know the boy or girl well, that he or she is less at ease playing with same-age peers than socializing with older people where the only child can act grown-up or with younger children where the only child can act in the older role. "Coming up in a world of adults, I grew up too fast in some ways to enjoy the company of people my own age. They kept wanting to do a lot of childish things, and I felt too grown-up to want to fool with that."

It is easy for parents to forget that although socially mature, their only son or daughter is still a child in need of the unrestricted, thoughtless, carefree freedom that is part of a healthy growing up. *Freedom from adult responsibility* is a playful side of what a childhood is about. To give oneself over to fun and games and adventure, without having to worry about acting mature like parents, allows the boy or girl to develop his or her childish side.

Therefore, although still valuing the adult-like qualities of their only child, parents can encourage this important freedom from responsibility by adequately socializing him or her with other children the same age. The only child cannot learn to act his or her age by associating with adults. The boy or girl must be given opportunity to interact with peers.

Pitfalls for the Child: Assuming Too Much Blame

For some only children, "I'm sorry" is an automatic response when anything goes wrong in the family, whether the boy or girl actually had anything to do with it or not. "Because I was the primary focus of attention in the family,

I just assumed that if my parents weren't happy, it must be because of me. If I was okay, they were okay; at least, that's the message I got. So if they weren't okay, then something must be the matter with me. Something about the way I was or something I did. Then it was my responsibility to own up and make the family feel better." So, when tired parents at the end of a long day bicker out their tensions with each other, the only child may interrupt: "I'm sorry, what did I do wrong?" Then the child may try to cheer everybody up.

To moderate the only child's tendency to assume responsibility for parental unhappiness or misfortune, it helps if parents keep clarifying the separation of responsibility for individual actions and emotional well-being. For example: suppose the child is slow getting ready and delays the family's departure for a movie. Hurrying to get there on time, the driving parent gets a speeding ticket along the way. When the parent gets angry for getting caught, the only child may automatically apologize. "I'm sorry. It's all my fault! If I hadn't dawdled, you wouldn't have tried to beat the light, been stopped by the police, and ended up feeling so bad."

In this situation, parents need to help the child learn to adequately separate responsibility. They can explain that dawdling was the child's responsibility, but driving was up to the parent. The first instance did not create the second. Association between the two events does not constitute causation. That's the point: *the automatically apologetic only child needs to be continually reminded that he or she is not the sole cause of happiness or unhappiness in the family, nor of all things going right or going wrong.*

28

~~~~~~

OBLIGATION

STRENGTHS FROM INDEBTEDNESS

D espite the appearance of being spoiled with all the attention and indulgence parents have to give, most only children do *not* grow up carefree. Despite the appearance of having it easy with just a single child to manage, most parents of only children do *not* operate under less pressure of responsibility than parents of multiple children. In fact, in most of these families, parents and child all labor under some degree of obligation to each other. Neither being parents to an only child nor the only child to parents are roles to be taken lightly. Each feels committed to do well by the other.

Sense of responsibility and sense of obligation are not the same, although the second can easily develop from the first as it often does in only child families. *Responsibility has to do with ownership*, making independent decisions and agreeing to cope with the consequences for good or ill. *Obligation has to do with indebtedness*, honoring what is owed to others and feeling the need to pay them back.

Because parents and the only child are often grateful for what each has received from the other, a sense of mutual indebtedness can develop early in their family relationship. "It isn't just love that keeps me and my parents so close, it's a sense of duty. I feel like I owe them so much, and they feel the same way about me." *In many only child families, there is the feeling of promises to keep and debts to be repaid.*

The child, for example, may resolve: "Since I am the one and only child they have, I *should:*

- turn out well,
- make them proud,
- make them happy,
- carry on the family line,
- remain the center of their world,
- repay them for all they have invested,
- take care of them when they are sick or old,
- make sure holidays and special occasions go well,
- and keep in contact after leaving home so they don't get lonely."

On their side, parents may have their own set of resolves: "Since this is the one and only child we have, we *should:*

- make our child happy,
- help our child to succeed,
- sacrifice for our child to get ahead,
- include our child in our adult world,
- notice when anything is going wrong,
- protect our child from possible dangers,
- avoid making mistakes that would harm our child,
- and support our child's development in every way we can."

Although parents and multiple children might subscribe to many of these statements about each other, they are not likely to do so with as much sense of obligation as parents and the only child. In some only child families, the sense of duty can seem almost contractual: *parents should provide and protect, and the only child should please and perform.*

Obligation Can Beget Conscientiousness

From feelings of obligation nurtured in their family, many only children tend to develop a strong sense of personal obligation toward themselves, particularly around matters of work performance. There is a quality of taking themselves seriously that becomes apparent, for example, when in upper elementary school or junior high they are, in company with a group of other students, assigned a common project for a grade.

In this situation, certain qualities frequently emerge:

- getting everyone organized,
- keeping everyone focused on the task,
- asserting leadership and taking charge,
- setting and overseeing a schedule of completion,
- finishing up what other team members leave undone,
- and attending to the quality of production to make sure the project is up to acceptable standards.

This kind of obligatory response often characterizes the only child's approach to a task in the workplace as an adult— *being very conscientious* and *wanting to do a job well.*

This conscientiousness can contribute to the only child's code of self-reliance in ways parents can support. For example, the only child often feels *obliged:*

- to finish what he or she starts (*to follow through to completion*),
- to keep promises to self and others (*to meet commitments*),
- to maintain continuity of effort in support of significant resolves (*to maintain consistency*),
- to make a decision even when it's hard choosing either way (*to reach closure*),
- to own responsibility for the outcome of personal choices made (*to face personal consequences*).

By meeting these demands of conscientiousness, the only child is treating himself or herself seriously.

The same is true when it comes to wanting to perform a task well. Work is not something people do external to themselves. It is an expression of themselves, and it reflects how they treat themselves. Thus, someone who acts uncaring about his or her work is essentially acting uncaring of himself or herself in the process.

By caring how they do, by honoring this sense of obligation to discharge a responsibility or do a task well, only children honor themselves. "Sure, I want to do well to please my parents, but mostly I want to do well to please myself. I feel I owe it to myself to do my level best." Work is not a casual commitment.

One of the great strengths of many only children is that by feeling that they should take themselves seriously, act conscientiously, and do a task well, they are honoring a personal obligation to treat themselves with respect. In this, they are usually like their mother and father who take their parenting very seriously, and who want to do their "level best" as well.

29

RISKS FROM OBLIGATION

THE BURDEN OF GUILT

The greatest vulnerability from obligation that parents and the only child feel is *guilt* for failing to do their duty to each other. The more that obligation governs their relationship ("I must do well to make my parents look good," "We must do everything we can to support our child's interests"), the more susceptibility to guilt there is for everyone. At worst, the only child family in which obligation has been enthroned dictates a set of terms that are hard to live with for everyone.

- *There can be a rule-ridden code of personal and interpersonal conduct governed by a host of unforgiving shoulds.* "Of course we loved each other, but we weren't really free to love each other. Even now, after all these years, when I see my parents, I am always asking myself: How *ought* I to act? What *ought* I to say? And I believe they probably are asking themselves the same questions when they see me."
- *There can be an earnest desire to do things "right" so as not to be in the "wrong."* "It's the hardest part of these teenage years. Here we are trying to do what we believe is for the best, only to be angrily told that we are worse than any other parents. It just kills us to be told we are making nothing but mistakes, when all we want to do is keep our child safe and well."

- *There can be extreme sensitivity to criticism from each other for fear of being found wanting or at fault.* "I hate being corrected by my parents because then I get down on myself. What they think of me matters so much! That's why I get angry, to cover up my hurt. Blaming them for blaming me. And then they get hurt, because they can't stand my criticism either. We all try so hard to do right that we hate being told that we did wrong."

Manipulating Guilt

Another vulnerability that parents and the only child have from the obligation between them is a susceptibility to having their guilt from obligation manipulated by the other party to get his or her way. Thus, the only child, thwarted by parental refusal for what he or she wants, angrily charges: "You never let me have anything; you just don't love me, and I don't love you!" and begins to cry. Can parents hold their stand in this face of such cruel beliefs and obvious suffering? If not, if they give in to this *emotional extortion* and allow the child to get his or her way, their susceptibility to guilt will be played upon to destructive effect. Then, over time, resentment at allowing this manipulation will injure their trust and caring in the relationship.

The same is true when parents, to get their adolescent only child to stay home with them instead of going out to socialize with friends, pull the strings of guilt to get their way. "You never spend any time with us. You treat us like we just don't matter to you anymore. But if that's the way you feel, then just go out and have a good time. We'll stay home by ourselves. Alone." Now both parents look hurt and forlorn to drive home their implied statement of suffering. Is the child going to be able to pull away? If so, not without feeling torn and hurt and angry.

Instead of either parents or child manipulating the other's guilt to get their way, all are better served by making a direct declaration of needs. "This is what I would like to have happen and why."

Divorce and Guilt

For parents, divorce (see Part Nine, beginning on page 159) can empower their guilt in an extremely unhealthy way when one or both decide to *compensate* the child for the hurt that separation of the marriage has inflicted. For them, divorce represents not just a severing of the parents' marital commitment to each other, but of their joint familial commitment to the child. It is guilt for breaking this second commitment that can drive parents into making it up to their child by saying "yes" too often (excessive indulgence) and "no" not enough (inadequate restraint) in order to please at all costs. "I have caused my child too much suffering already. I can't stand to see her suffer anymore."

Responsible and Compensatory Guilt

Divorced parents of an only child need to distinguish between *responsible guilt* and *compensatory guilt,* or else the latter may cause them to forsake making healthy demands for responsibility and setting healthy limits over freedom.

- Responsible guilt means that each divorced parent, particularly the one who initiated the divorce, accepts that one consequence of separating the marriage is to cause profound hurt to the only child. By this decision, his or her secure world of family is torn apart by the two adults the child loves most dearly. In recognition of this cost, it is normal and healthy for parents to experience responsible guilt: "By our self-serving actions, we are causing suffering to our child." *It is up to parents to admit this culpability.*
- Compensatory guilt is of the lasting kind. It exacts ongoing tribute from divorced parents who feel they must continue to punish themselves and continue to make special reparation to the child for the damage they have done. Unhappily,

compensatory guilt is self-perpetuating. Each payment they make only confirms how much they owe. The burden of guilt gets heavier, not lighter. *To end compensatory guilt, parents must find a way to forgive themselves.*

Eliminating "Should" and "Ought"

To keep terms of obligation from becoming unduly oppressive, parents might want to consider omitting two words when discussing with their child what they want and don't want to happen: the words "should" and "ought." Both words just encourage more obligation than the only child already feels he or she has. For both parents and the only child, a sense of mutual obligation is deeply ingrained and neither needs to carry any more.

In addition, there are certain common parental statements, usually made in frustration, that can well be avoided:

- "You've really let us down!"
- "How could you do this to us?"
- "You should be ashamed of how you've acted!"
- "You never think of any needs except your own!"
- "Have you ever considered what you owe us?"
- "After all we've done for you, is this the thanks we get?"
- "Someday you'll feel sorry for how you've treated us!"
- "Now that you're on your own, we don't matter anymore!"

Statements like these, which charge the only child with failing in his or her obligation to parents, arouse guilt at first but cause resentment later. "That's one thing I'll never forgive my parents for—punishing me with guilt when I didn't measure up to their expectations or simply didn't do what they wanted."

Invoke obligation often enough and parents can actually end up alienating the affection of the child they love.

30

~~~~~~

INDIVIDUALITY

STRENGTHS FROM BEING DIFFERENT

B ecause of the undiluted family focus they receive, only
children are closely noticed by their parents. Ever vigilant to the subtle signs of something wrong, these parents are quick to seek help when their son or daughter is
feeling unwell or otherwise appears troubled. All other factors being equal, parents tend to request more incidental
medical attention for a first child because their inexperience
and anxiety has not been lessened by exposure to the common ailments and complaints of preceding children.

This same undiluted focus on the only child also fills
parents with a sense of wonder they usually cannot replicate
with multiple children. The only child (and the first child for
awhile) captivates a quality of parental attention, arouses
feelings of parental infatuation, and receives an amount of
parental time, which are unrivaled. "We love watching every
little step in our child's growth. We don't want to miss a
thing. And we try to give every encouragement we can."

It is this extreme parental responsiveness that draws
the only child out, nurturing and supporting the boy's or girl's
individual character, interests, and capacities, to a degree
that subsequent children are far less likely to receive. In
addition, because there are no siblings in the family with
whom to compete, the only child is given an open field to
self-define on many of his or her own terms. The parents
themselves can afford to be more flexible with an only child

than when there is a multiplicity of children to manage. In all these ways, only children are encouraged to become fully themselves by parents who support as many facets of the child's individuality as they can. *Because of this parental investment, only children often have the opportunity to develop more dimensions of themselves than multiple children living in a single family.*

Clarity, Conviction, and Integrity

The strengths from individuality in the only child are many.

- From all the affirmation of his or her individuality received at home, the only child develops a strong sense of *clarity*—of clear preferences, dislikes, values, and beliefs about the world. "Sometimes it feels like I was born with my mind made up. I can't remember not knowing what was true and what was right and what I wanted. I may not be that confident getting along with others, but I am certain about who I am and what I like."
- Clarity encourages a strong sense of *conviction*, with the only child wed to his or her personal beliefs. "When I make up my own mind, I don't change it."
- Conviction encourages the child to act with *integrity*. The only child can be unwilling to compromise or sacrifice for the sake of fitting in or getting along with others. "Why should I give up being who I am just to get along with other people?"

Strengthening Individuality

The first way that parents can affirm the strengths from individuality in their son or daughter is by affirming the three traits—clarity, conviction, and integrity—that tend to develop in the only child. This affirmation is not as simple as it sounds, however, because sometimes such strong self-definition can prove difficult for parents to honor.

- *Clarity* may cause the only child to speak openly about feelings, opinions, and concerns that parents may find discomforting to hear: "I wake up at night with the strangest dreams; do you think I'm crazy?"
- *Conviction* may cause the only child to stubbornly adhere to beliefs that he or she wishes would change: "I've decided it's cruel to kill animals, so I will no longer eat meat."
- *Integrity* may cause the only child to act on principles no matter what the cost: "I'm not going to change what I wrote in my paper just to satisfy the teacher."

This strong commitment to individuality can cause many only children to become adherents of the belief: "To thine own self be true." A social corollary to this belief that many only children hold is: "What other people will think about me matters less than being who and how I am." Many only children are not intimidated by the eyes of the world (of social disapproval) because they feel so well accepted by parents.

Even parents can become impatient, however, with a strong show of individuality by their only child at home. In their frustration, they can be tempted to shut the child's strong opinion down. In general, they are best advised *not* to reject clarity ("Don't say that!"), *not* to criticize conviction ("How can you think like that?"), and *not* to punish integrity ("Don't tell me I am wrong; go to your room!")

As for those times when parents see the only child asserting individuality *out in the world* to his or her personal disadvantage, they can help the boy or girl at least reckon the social costs. "Of course the decision is up to you, but it seems to us that when you refuse to join the game unless you are given the position you want, then the other children may not want to have you on their team."

In support of this commitment to his or her individuality, the only child often develops a streak of *willfulness*.

A strongly self-defined only child, whose sense of individuality has been nourished by parental encouragement and acceptance, tends

- to be outspoken,
- to be self-regulated,
- to be insistent,
- to be stubborn,
- to be controlling,
- and to be committed to getting one's way.

Individuality and Androgyny

Part of the only child's individuality also comes from a dual identification with both parents. Instead of taking after one more than the other, the only child tends to incorporate traits from both. Often irrespective of sex role stereotyping, "male" and "female" characteristics become incorporated in the child who can seem *androgynous* to some degree. "I'm like both my parents, but in different ways. And that's how I want to be—a dreamer like my mom, and practical like my dad."

Supporting the only child's androgyny can sometimes be difficult for parents who are more narrowly self-defined. The thing for parents to remember is that the child wants to be like *both* of them. Therefore, enforcing adherence to stereotypical single sex traits (male = rough and adventurous, for example; female = sensitive and supportive, for example) not only restricts the child's growth but rejects some part of the child's connection to the opposite sex parent. It is better to allow the only child to claim identification with both parents.

31

RISKS FROM INDIVIDUALITY

NOT FITTING IN

Three common risks from the only child's strong sense of individuality are: *personal entitlement* (the belief that his or her individuality confers special status and deserves special treatment), *older identification* (subscribing to values and norms more associated with his or her parent's generation than with peers), and *eccentricity* (becoming so used to living on individual terms, that he or she significantly departs from social norms).

- Problems with *personal entitlement* can cause the only child to act like he or she is better than others and so deserves exceptions from rules. Just as special arrangements were made in response to the child's individuality at home, the boy or girl may expect similar adaptation by the world. Thus, when the elementary teacher won't allow the only child extra time to finish a classroom assignment, the boy or girl may consider this unfair, believing that his or her uniqueness should be accommodated by the system: "I should be given more time to get work done if that is what I need!"

- Problems with *older identification* can cause the only child to embrace a set of cultural norms more associated with the parental generation than with his or her own.

113

Used to being treated like a "little adult" or an "adult child," the boy or girl has no older or younger siblings in the family to provide a contemporary sense of the world from a youthful perspective. Adopting the parental perspective, the only child can feel out of step with peers: "I feel I have more in common with adults than with people my own age."

- Problems with *eccentricity* can cause the only child to follow such an individual path, and develop such an individual identity, that the boy or girl feels socially set apart, unable to find many peers who can accept this degree of differentness, or who are similar enough to want to make a friendship. A sense of being solitary can be one result: "All my life I've been kind of a misfit, too into my self to be understood by others or to want to be part of their groups. More of a loner than a joiner."

It is all right for parents to adjust a lot of family functioning to suit the only child's individual needs (delaying family outings because the child wants to finish a project, for example), as long as they make it clear that in the outside world the boy or girl is *not* going to be *entitled* to similar treatment. Thus, in anticipation of the child entering school, parents make it very clear that classroom membership has certain requirements, more strict than those at home, that they expect the child to learn to meet. The message that parents may want to give is: *"Although it is true that at home you are one and only, out in the world you are one of many."*

The most powerful way to moderate the problem of *older identification* is by parents adequately socializing the only child's life with enough social exposure to same-age acquaintances and friends. To remain sufficiently identified with other children, the only child must have significant ongoing contact with peers. The message that parents may want to give is: *"Although we love the grown-up ways you act with us, we also want you to enjoy the fun of growing up with friends your own age."*

When the only child appears resolved to march to such a different drummer that he or she is at risk of appearing *eccentric*, perhaps becoming more self-preoccupied and solitary, parents can affirm this strong expression of individuality and still encourage social membership. Sense of uniqueness does not have to carry with it a sentence of social isolation. Often this encouragement requires parents to push the child into groups he or she is not inclined to join—at church, at school, in sports—in order to create opportunities for social exposure and affiliation that the boy or girl would otherwise not seek. The message that parents may want to give is: *"Although we are glad you have a strong sense of yourself and enjoy being by yourself, we also want you to be able to enjoy a sense of belonging with others."*

32

~~~~~~

EXTREMES

STRENGTHS FROM HIGH DEMANDS

With two or more children, parents usually accept that they cannot provide everything for all their kids; but with only one, there can be an irresistible temptation to try. In consequence, these parents can tend to be *extremely* conscientious, *extremely* vigilant, *extremely* supportive, *extremely* giving, and *extremely* dedicated to the boy's or girl's emotional well-being, development of interests, educational advancement, and performance success.

Because of this extreme parental commitment, the only child can be driven to extremes in response—feeling *extremely* responsible for parents, *extremely* sensitive to their moods; and striving to be *extremely* pleasing, *extremely* grown-up, and *extremely* good at school. What is created by this convergence of extremes is a constant pressure from one side of the relationship to live up to the standard of effort set by the other. For either party to fail in their resolve would be to feel derelict in the relationship.

The Question That Motivates Extreme Behavior
In the process, parents and the only child can be plagued by the same problematic question: *"What is enough?"* What is considerate enough, what is contributing enough, what is working hard enough, what is achieving enough, what is pleasing enough, what is giving enough return to satisfy the sense of obligation built into this highly invested relationship?

In many instances, there is a sense of deficiency on one or both sides. "No matter how hard I try, sometimes I feel I'm not doing enough to make my child happy." "No matter how hard I try, sometimes I feel I'm not doing enough to please my parents." *"Enough" seems always out of reach.* The answer to "What is enough?" can often be giving more and trying harder until only extremes will do:

- Excess rules out moderation ("Our child is worth spending more on than we can afford");
- Superiority rules out the ordinary ("I must be better than others to make my parents proud");
- Excellence rules out being average ("I must be perfect or I'll let my parents down");
- All rules out some ("We must develop all of our child's interests and talents").

The great strength and vulnerability of the relationship between parents and the only child is wanting to do so well by the other.

Strength of Dedication

In most cases, deciding to have an only child is not a casual choice. Thoughtfully made, the decision is carried out with a sense of dedication that invests an enormous amount of parental energy over time. The immediate outcome of this seriousness of purpose and constancy of commitment is that *the only child tends to be extremely well parented.*

Firmly bonded to parents, growing up under unwavering surveillance, the only child knows what is expected, is well supported, and is continually encouraged to increase his or her capacities in esteem-filling ways. Like any other parents, the parents of an only child can make mistakes, but these decisions are not usually the outcome of carelessness or neglect. Parents of an only child hold themselves to high account, and their son or daughter as well, who usually develops ambitious self-expectations in response.

Strength of Supervision

One of the great strengths of extremes for parents of an only child is their *supervision of detail*. With multiple children, much can escape parental notice. In addition, some parental resolves are not consistently kept up, some good intentions are not carried through, and some requirements are not uniformly enforced, because when managing so many children, some slippage is bound to occur. "Having three kids, there's no way we can stay on top of everything all the time."

With an undistracted parental focus on the only child, however, the boy or girl feels closely watched. "It's like being under a microscope, sometimes. That's why I'd like to have another child in the family. To take some of their attention off me." Although only children like receiving a lot of notice, even they can reach their limits, particularly during adolescence (see Part Eight, beginning on page 127) when tolerance for parental oversight and surveillance becomes reduced as the desire for freedom and independence naturally increases.

In fact, one of the strengths of these parents is maintaining extreme (and often unpopular) watchfulness over their only child as he or she grows through the challenges and risks of the teenage years. They remain fluent with the surveillance questions: "*Where* are you going, *how* will you get there, *who* will you be with, *what* will you be doing, *when* will you return, and *why* can't you tell us?" They require reliable answers before permission is given.

The "Small" Stuff

Driven by extremes, parents of only children also tend to ignore a well-intentioned but often ill-advised piece of guidance: "Don't sweat the small stuff." What this counsel suggests is that parents can get so caught up in pursuing their child about daily details that they risk overreacting when slight omissions occur (once again a chore is sloppily accomplished) and lose sight of the larger issues (like the child's emotional and social well-being.) In fact, the small stuff is well worth "sweating," and parents of an only child tend to be well equipped for this extremely demanding part of their job.

What is small stuff? Examples include a myriad of behaviors that parents often want to teach their child:

- cleaning up any messes made,
- putting back what has been taken out,
- returning what is borrowed,
- answering when asked a question,
- listening when spoken to,
- doing chores without reminders,
- telling the whole story about what happened,
- being on time,
- following directions,
- speaking courteously,
- honoring agreements,

and a host of other small daily observances that are extremely important to pursue for two reasons.

1. When parents invest the energy and take the time to "sweat the small stuff," the only child knows they are not about to let the "big stuff" go—such as not keeping up adequate school performance, not obeying laws, or violating significant household rules. A powerful message is communicated to the child when parents refuse to let the small stuff go: "We mean to monitor your conduct both in small and large ways."

2. When parents realize that no "small stuff" is ever really small, they are recognizing a larger reality:

every behavior of their child that they supervise has both *specific* and *symbolic* value. Making sure that the child tells the whole story about what happened (specific value) can represent an importance parents place on *honesty* (symbolic value). Making sure that the child uses courtesy in conversation can represent an importance parents place on *consideration*. Making sure that the child honors agreements can represent an importance parents place on *reliability*. Making sure that the child cleans and picks up after making a mess can represent an importance parents place on *responsibility*. Small stuff signifies larger meanings that contribute to the traits and qualities of character that the only child can be encouraged to develop. "We keep after you to listen when we talk, and we try our best to listen to you, because we believe that listening shows *respect*."

Proactive Parenting

The extreme degree of focus that parents bring to bear on their only child allows them a luxury, and endows them with a strength that parents of multiple children often lack: *time and inclination to be proactive in their parenting by thinking about the big picture of their child's growth.* The more children in a family, the more parents tend to become reactive to demands in the present. After all, it's hard to think about how to nurture your children's future development when coping takes precedence over planning—one child is sick and feverish in bed; the other two, fighting over what to watch on TV, show early signs of contracting the ailment that has felled the first.

Parents of an only child can usually afford to be more reflective and deliberate in their parenting. They can take time to consider the discrepancy between how competent their young child is now and the greater competence that will be required when he or she leaves their care. They can be proactive in preparing him or her for adult self-sufficiency by gradually increasing their *assignment of responsibility* to the child, systematically encouraging growth toward adult independence (see Key 26). Because they watch their child so closely, parents can also increase the boy's or girl's self-understanding with the sensitive feedback they provide. The child becomes the beneficiary of their extreme observation: "Since my parents know me so well, a lot of times what they have to say helps me to better know myself." The reverse also applies. Parents are frequently the beneficiaries of insightful (though not always welcome) comments by their extremely observant only child.

33

RISKS FROM EXTREMES

OVERINVESTING AND DEFICIENCY BELIEFS

The parents' natural tendency to strive to do enough for their only child can be intensified by a number of factors in the parents' lives.

- Early deprivation of basic needs or other hardship in their family of origin can cause parents to want to compensate with their child for their experience. In consequence, they may want to provide in excess to the child to make up for their own lingering suffering. "I want to make sure our child never has to do without the stability and security that was not given to me."
- Death of a previous only child may cause parents to invest more heavily in the next child to help heal their pain and recover from the loss. In consequence, they may treat the new child partly as a replacement, wanting him or her to fulfill some possibilities of the child who died. "Our only child is a constant reminder of the one we lost, a second chance at parenting that the death of our first child denied."
- Although planning to have multiple children, a couple may be medically informed that one is all they can hope to conceive, and perhaps not without risk. Stopped short of having the larger family they wanted, one child becomes the only chance at parenting they get, the focus of all their

dreams. In consequence, the varied satisfactions available from having several children are sought from the only child. "Our daughter is going to be everything we ever wanted in a child."

- To restore closeness in a union that has become estranged because it lacks a center, partners may hope that having a son or daughter will renew their marriage. Somehow this child is supposed to bring reconciliation. In consequence, pressure is placed on the boy or girl to do more than make them parents. His or her addition is expected to recover the marriage as well. "Sharing a common love for our son is what we need to bring us closer together."
- By wanting the child to accomplish their unfulfilled dreams, disappointed parents may become preoccupied with pushing that son or daughter to do what they could not. In consequence, they risk sacrificing the child's independence on the altar of their own frustrated ambitions. "I want my child to achieve what I could not."

Even without the added impetus of these special circumstances, parental investment in the only child is always at some risk of creating high expectations and demands that can drive the only child to extremes in response. He or she can become continually troubled by mulling over endless variations of that agonizing question *"What is enough?"*

- "What is functioning well enough?"
- "What is being ideal enough?"
- "What is achieving enough?"
- "What is being pleasing enough?"
- "What is acting grateful enough?"

Deficiency Beliefs of Children

Vulnerability to these anxious questions is increased by the accusatory answers the only child can provide. He or she may respond by constructing a cruel set of internal beliefs about his or her inadequacy. These *deficiency beliefs* can set the terms on which the child comes to live within himself or herself, the terms on which the child lives with parents and significant others, and the terms that dictate how he or she relates to the larger world.

- In response to the question "What is functioning well enough?" the child may feel deficient and diagnostically conclude: *"There is something wrong with me for not always being competent in what I do."*
- In response to the question "What is being ideal enough?" the child may feel deficient and critically conclude: *"I am a failure for not being perfect."*
- In response to the question "What is achieving enough?" the child may feel deficient and disappointedly conclude: *"No matter how I strive, I will never be a success."*
- In response to the question "What is being pleasing enough?" the child may feel deficient and dejectedly conclude: *"There's no way for me to ever satisfy my parents."*
- In response to the question "What is acting grateful enough?" the child may feel deficient and guiltily conclude: *"I can never repay my parents for all they've done for me."*

Such deficiency beliefs continually criticize efforts and attack self-esteem. At best, the occasional triumph brings only momentary relief because it is seen as an exception to the rule. "Sure, I got 98 percent on the exam, but that just shows how far below that score I usually achieve." Deficiency beliefs can cause the only child to dismiss or discount performance data to the contrary.

Proving Loops

More important, the only child who feels tempted by extremes often acts to make a hard situation worse. By trying to prove that these painful beliefs about personal inadequacy are invalid, the child just affirms what he or she was hoping to deny. "I keep wanting to prove I'm okay, but no matter how hard I try or how well I do, I end up feeling worse about myself. What's the matter with me?" The answer is: by acting to disprove a negative personal belief, he or she just affirms that the underlying charge of inadequacy must to some degree be true. Self-esteem is anchored in the opposing conviction. "I have nothing to prove. I am acceptable, sufficient, and worthwhile just the way I am."

What Parents Model Is What They Teach

When extremely conscientious parents see their only child pushed into unhappiness by these deficiency beliefs, they may urge the boy or girl not to be so hard on himself or herself, even offering themselves as a negative example to avoid. "We've always put too much pressure on ourselves. Never being satisfied. No room for mistakes. It's not a happy way to be. We can speak from experience. Don't be like us!"

What these well-meaning parents don't understand, however, is that their primary source of influence is not through what they say, but by what they model—by who and how they are. They instruct by example. The only child learns to strive for extremes from parents who are driven by their own excessive responses to variations of the same vexing question: *"What is enough?"*

Deficiency Beliefs of Parents

In answer, parents have their own set of deficiency beliefs, all part of a larger one: "Because we do not always please, prepare, protect, and provide for our child, we are inadequate as parents." Having slipped into this unhappy frame of mind, it doesn't help them when their adolescent complains that teenage friends have better parents than they. Feeling relatively deprived, the teenager charges: "Other parents give their kids more than you give me!" It is a no-win situation. The more parents give, the more the only child's expectations may be raised, and the more dissatisfied the teenager can become. "You never let me do anything. You just don't care!"

Determining What Is Enough

To avoid the temptation of extremes, and to diminish the development of deficiency beliefs that they engender, parents need to examine

- their personal *goals* (how high is enough?),
- their personal *standards* (how well is enough?),
- and their personal *limits* (how much is enough?).

If they believe that only *achieving the best with their child* is good enough, that only *maintaining perfection in their parenting* is doing well enough, and that only *doing everything their child demands* is sufficient enough, they are expecting too much.

Personal goals, standards, and limits set many of the fundamental terms on which people live within themselves and with others. Not genetically determined, they are chosen. Many parents of an only child would benefit from choosing to relax some of these terms a little. These parents could justify doing so by having confidence that with only a single child to raise, they are well intended, committed, and positioned to do a good job with that beloved son or daughter. They do not need to resort to extremes. A good faith effort will suffice. To moderate their inclinations, these parents may want to remind themselves of the following *sufficiency beliefs:*

- *A mixed performance* is the best that most parents and their child can give most of the time.
- *Ordinary efforts by parents* generally suffice—they do not have to give their all to give enough.
- *Receiving some of what he or she needs and wants* is usually adequate to ensure the child's healthy growth.

34

‸‸

ADOLESCENCE

WHEN THE HARD HALF OF PARENTING BEGINS

Many parents of an only child are woefully unprepared for their son's or daughter's adolescence. They do not anticipate that their cooperative and communicative little companion is going to grow through some of the normal resistant, more private, and socially separate changes that usually begin somewhere between the ages of nine and thirteen.

It is not uncommon for parents to innocently contribute to the intensity of their only child's adolescence by the parenting they have previously given. In their loving efforts to help their only child to grow by encouraging entitlement, assertiveness, and influence within the family, they may empower more adolescent willfulness, opposition, and independence than they are at first prepared to handle.

When Adolescence Comes As a Surprise

"It's just that we've been so close and got along so well. We never imagined our child would want to keep us from knowing what was going on, would disagree and argue so, would object to us as parents, and wouldn't want to spend time with us! What have we done wrong? What's wrong with our child?" *Usually nothing is wrong, except the unpreparedness of parents.*

What can help prevent this surprise is having sufficient knowledge of child development so parents do not treat the

127

process of adolescence as a punishable offense. It really makes a difference when parents do not blame themselves or their only child for changes that are no one's fault but are part of a normal process of transformation. The boy's or girl's sense of self-definition and dependency on family is becoming permanently altered. When parents have some understanding of this revolutionary period of change (why it is, some of the common quandaries it is likely to create), a powerful advantage is gained: *perspective*. They are able to place the child's new behaviors into a coherent pattern of larger growth. They do *not* take the child's changes personally.

With this understanding, motivations typically governing the adolescent's behavior (like social independence, assertion of individual differentness, freedom for experimentation, enjoyment of argument, opposition to rules and limits, and fascination with risk) can be accepted by parents who then direct their energies toward helping the teenager make constructive decisions during a challenging period of his or her life.

Thus, although they may refuse to let their *mid-adolescent* freshman in high school stay out until 3 A.M., they understand the desire for grown-up freedom motivating such a request at this stage, as well as the anger they receive for saying "no." By having a larger context in which to place this more difficult period of growth, parents can normalize their expectations about some of the changes to come, reducing the likelihood of being caught off guard and overreacting in response.

If their *early adolescent* begins to let homework slide in upper elementary school, they are prepared for this possibility. They understand how, at this stage, opposing authority reflects a common antipathy to being told what to do. They stand ready, however, to weigh in with their supervision by insisting that, like it or not, the boy or girl *will* still get his or her assignments done. They do not stand idly by and allow the adolescent to rebel against his or her own self-interests by failing to perform up to capacity. After all, maintaining adequate school achievement is one important pillar of self-esteem.

Thankless Parenting

For parents of an only child, the period of adolescence can be one of *thankless parenting* when they take increasingly unpopular stands for their beloved child's best interests against what he or she urgently wants or thinks is fair. At the time, they do not receive appreciation from their child for the loyal opposition they provide. Quite the contrary, their son or daughter often takes offense: "You just don't love me, that's why you won't let me go!" Reply the parents: "It's *because* we love you that we're saying 'no.'"

Adolescence is a mutually offensive process because it continually places parents and teenager in opposition. A healthy teenager pushes for all the freedom he or she can get as soon as he or she can get it because, ultimately, achieving independence is what adolescence is about. Healthy parents restrain this push within the limits of safety and responsibility because they know that permissiveness is no protection.

This *conflict of interests* unfolds over the eight to ten years of adolescence, creating an ongoing abrasion in the relationship that little by little wears down the dependence between them. Parents gradually turn over more decision making as the teenager demonstrates more competence to undertake that power on his or her own. Finally, at the end of adolescence, parents and the only child are able and willing to let go of one another and establish a functional independence between them. Parents are free at last from responsibility for their child, and the child finally accepts total responsibility for his or her freedom.

35

~~~~~~

STRENGTHS FROM ADOLESCENCE

ENERGIZING HEALTHY GROWTH

A healthy adolescence makes three vital contributions to the only child's growth:

1. It causes the girl or boy to reject being entirely defined and responded to as a child by desiring and demanding more adult standing and freedoms in the world: *"I want to act and be treated like I'm more grown-up."*
2. It causes the girl or boy to search for a sense of individual identity to some degree different from the child she or he was and from the parents she or he has: *"I want to be my own person."*
3. It causes the girl or boy to become more reliant on the company of peer relationships to achieve social independence from parents: *"I want to have my own family of friends."*

Each of these contributions cannot be made without incurring a psychological cost. To some degree, *stress* is placed upon their relationship as adolescence causes parents and the only child to grow apart. There is some sense of *loss* of the old companionship: "We spend less of our time together." There is some *anxiety* about how the new relationship will turn out to be: "With more friction between us, will we ever feel as close again?" Because this separation from childhood and from parents can be both painful and scary, there are times when all parties are called upon to be brave.

The Courage of Adolescence

Particularly for the only child, so powerfully bonded to parents, *adolescence is an act of courage.* She or he must pull away and push against parents for more independence, often courting disapproval and creating conflict for freedom's sake.

- The girl or boy asserts individuality. ("I am different now!")
- The girl or boy contests limits. ("It's not fair that you won't let me go!")
- The girl or boy wants social separation. ("I'd rather spend my time with friends!")
- The girl or boy experiments with risk to grow. ("Just because it's dangerous, doesn't mean that I'll get hurt!")

Although often cloaked in protective bravado ("I don't care what you think!"), the only child is often actually afraid.

- *The fear of individuality* is fear of rejection: "Suppose I become so different that my parents can no longer accept how I am changing?"
- *The fear of contesting limits* is fear of conflict: "Suppose I push so hard against my parents rules that I push their love away?"
- *The fear of social separation* is fear of estrangement: "Suppose friends become so important that closeness to them costs me closeness to my parents?"
- *The fear of experimentation* is fear of failure: "Suppose I try something new, get in trouble, and mess up my life?"

For parents, the adolescence of their only child requires courage too, and the name of that courage is *letting go.*

131

Because investment in their child is so high, preoccupation is so great, and attachment is so strong, release of their beloved son or daughter to more independence can arouse its own set of fears.

- *The fear of responsibility* is: "Suppose our child gets hurt from the freedoms we allow?"
- *The fear of estrangement* is: "Suppose our child becomes so different from us that we lose what we once had in common?"
- *The fear of alienation* is: "Suppose we take hard stands for our child's best interests that permanently cost us our child's love?"
- *The fear of abandonment* is: "Suppose our child becomes so attached to life with friends that time with us no longer matters?"

In answer to these questions, parents need to answer *fears* about "what if?" with *faith* in what has been, what is, and what will be.

- They need to keep faith in the bonding of childhood that has provided a strong foundation of love for their relationship, creating a secure attachment on which the child can depend.
- They need to keep faith in the love conveyed by their loyal opposition to the child's irresponsible wants during adolescence, defining a separation of interests while keeping them constantly connected through their communication over differences.
- And they need to keep faith that as their adolescent grows into his or her own individual person, they will be able to reconcile their value and lifestyle differences by creating a bond of acceptance that bridges the distinctions between them.

36

NURTURING STRENGTHS FROM ADOLESCENCE

ENCOURAGING RESPONSIBILITY, DIVERSITY, AND COMMUNITY

P arents can do much to nurture the three contributions of adolescence to their only child's development.

- They can support the child's desire to act more grown-up by encouraging *additional responsibility.* As opposed to saying, "We'll take care of everything for you," they can now say, "The time has come to learn to do more for yourself."

- They can support the child's desire to be his or her own person by accepting more *diversity of growth.* As opposed to saying, "Don't change from the child we have always loved," they can now say, "The time has come to grow in new and different ways."

- They can support the child's desire to build *a social community independent of parents.* As opposed to saying, "Don't make friendships that take you away from us," they can now say, "The time has come for you to participate in more activities and groups outside of the family."

Responsibility

Strengthening power of responsibility during adolescence begins by transferring some of their traditional responsibility for the child to the child. Once the boy or girl, through words and actions, shows signs of separating from childhood by asserting differentness ("I'm not a little child anymore!" "I'm not the same as you!" "I don't have to act the way you want!"), then parents need to begin shifting responsibility to the early adolescent to support the growing independence he or she desires.

From this point on, the best protection that the teenager will have out in the world is being able to responsibly take care of himself or herself. To begin this transfer of responsibility to the young adolescent, parents can announce some of the changes they will be making so the growing boy or girl is not caught totally by surprise and understands their motivation.

- Where parents may have rescued the only child from unhappy consequences of his or her decision making, now they tell the young adolescent: "We expect you to admit your bad choices, take the consequences, learn from your errors, and right the situation the best you can, because *recovery from mistakes* is one important responsibility that goes with becoming more independent."

- Where parents may have jumped in and solved the only child's problems out in the world, now they delay giving their advice, telling the young adolescent: "Before we give you our suggestions, we expect you to figure out your own strategy for solving this difficulty because *problem solving* is one important responsibility that goes with becoming more independent."

- Where parents may have provided emotional support to fix the only child's feelings when unhappy, hurt, or otherwise upset, now they tell the young adolescent: "Increasingly you need to take care of your own emotional well-being, finding ways to get yourself feeling better when you are feeling bad because *emotional self-support* is one important responsibility that goes with becoming more independent."

As the young adolescent pushes for more freedom, parents need to push the only child to assume certain responsibilities in return, holding their son or daughter accountable for *consistency, predictability, and believability*. In doing so, they can make a statement of contract that might go as follows:

"Our willingness to give you more freedom of choice over your conduct depends upon our trust for putting you *at risk* of your own decision making. To take that risk, we need three kinds of behavior from you—

- *Consistency.* For example, we need evidence that you are continuing to take care of business at school by maintaining your grades as well as taking care of business at home by doing your chores in a timely manner.
- *Predictability.* For example, we need evidence that you are keeping your agreements with us about where you are going, what you will be doing, and when you will return.
- *Believability.* For example, we need evidence that you are giving us adequate (accurate and complete) information on which we can base our parenting decisions about allowing you the independence you desire.

You give us these three kinds of evidence of responsibility, and we will risk giving you more of the freedom you want. Show us evidence to the contrary, and we will reduce your freedom until that evidence is forthcoming once again."

Diversity

Strengthening power of diversity during adolescence begins by parents expanding some of their tolerance for unfamiliar differences as the only child changes on four levels at once.

- *Characteristics* change as the boy or girl becomes physically larger and more mature, beginning to acquire grown-up looks.
- *Values* change as the boy or girl becomes more drawn to ideals, attitudes, and tastes defined in opposition to the adult world, distinguishing the new counterculture of the teenager from the old-fashioned culture of the parents.
- *Habits* change as the boy or girl subscribes to patterns of behavior—becoming more messy, or more private, or more argumentative, for example—that tend to make the boy or girl harder for parents to live with at home.
- *Wants* change as the boy or girl seeks to break out of the boundaries of childhood to gain experience from acting older, demanding social freedoms that are harder for parents to grant and restrain.

Tolerance for these differences does *not* mean giving in to everything the adolescent asks. Tolerance means:

1. *understanding and accepting these differences as a normal part of the diversity that adolescent growth creates;*
2. *taking stands to help the adolescent keep decisions prompted by this diversity within the limits of safety and responsibility;*
3. *and not rejecting the boy or girl for changes in characteristics, values, habits, and wants that growth from childhood to adulthood has ordained.*

Social Community

Strengthening the power of community during adolescence begins as parents become willing to share their only child with a world of relationships that do not include themselves. It also helps for them to have friendships that do not always include the boy or girl. To encourage this mutual social independence from family, social separation must first feel emotionally safe.

For example, the only child may not feel comfortable going off with friends if he or she feels *guilty* for leaving parents behind, or feels *disloyal* for liking to be with others more than them. Parents may be reluctant to socialize independently of their only child if he or she feels *abandoned* by their leaving, or feels *rejected* because they prefer the company of adult friends for awhile. Sometimes asocial parents for whom the family provides sufficient social interaction, or parents who refuse to socialize without their child, can discourage social independence in their son or daughter.

Involving the adolescent in multiple social circles—in the extended family, in a volunteer service group, in a youth group at church, in other organized activities or sports—sometimes requires some pushing if the only child is shy or otherwise reluctant. *Social isolation during adolescence, however, can be costly both for what the boy or girl gives up at the time and lacks in preparation for adulthood later on.*

- Being a valued group member can help support *a sense of self-esteem:* "I feel good being liked by other people."
- Being an integral part of a group can create *a sense of belonging:* "I have friends who understand and accept me."
- Participating in a group activity can create *a sense of contribution:* "Part of what we made was because of my ideas."
- Having like-minded friends to be with can build *a sense of community:* "When you have friends you don't have to be alone."
- Being able to maintain one's position in a group can provide *a sense of confidence:* "I know how to get along with other people."

Particularly for an only child, so comfortable socializing with parents who love companioning their child, creating an independent social world may seem unnecessary and less congenial than the satisfying relationships of family.

When this social indifference or reluctance carries over into adolescence, the child is often well served by being given a choice by parents. "We expect you to be part of some organized group activity outside of home and school. This is our decision. What that group is, however, you can select from the variety of options that we all come up with."

37

RISKS FROM
ADOLESCENCE

DIFFERENT RISKS AT DIFFERENT STAGES

Adolescence is that process of transformation that begins with the boy or girl pushing and pulling to loosen the ties of childhood dependency on parents, and ends eight to ten years later with the young person having learned enough responsibility to undertake independent self-support. One way to focus on risks in this process for parents and the only child is to consider it according to four different stages.

1. *Early adolescence* (typically occurring between ages nine and thirteen) is about *the change for the worse.* Dissatisfied with being defined and being treated as a child, the young boy or girl begins rejecting some old enjoyments and activities, and starts resisting some traditional family demands and limits that he or she previously accepted. Sometimes early adolescence coincides with the onset of puberty, but it does not have to. When it does, however, this first stage of adolescence tends to become more emotionally intensified.

   Now parents find the child increasingly negative and oppositional to live with, and frequently critical of them. More moody to be around, more easily upset, the early adolescent is less compliant and cooperative than of old. What is this change all about?

The boy or girl is breaking out of the boundaries of childhood to create more freedom to grow. At this early stage of the process, the child is more sure of how he or she *doesn't* want to be than how he or she *does* want to be: "I'm not interested in kid stuff anymore!" Not yet knowing how to replace valued activities that have been given up to mark this change, however, the boy or girl often suffers from a loss of self-esteem. Feeling disconnected from an old definition and not yet attached to a new one, he or she frequently acts bored, and restless: "I don't know what to do with myself!" The child was more secure and confident than is the early adolescent.

In the face of what often seems to be a sudden and unwelcome transformation in their only child (from positive to negative, from easy to difficult, from cooperative to resistant), parents are *vulnerable* to taking these growth changes personally. When they do, they may blame the child or themselves for the process of early adolescent change. "You used to be such a great kid, what happened to you?" "What have we done to cause you to act this way?"

Feeling hurt and rejected, they are at risk of expressing criticism back and doing injury to the child when he or she is at an extremely vulnerable stage—braving parental approval to start the painful process of separation that begins adolescent growing up.

2. *Mid-adolescence* (typically occurring between the ages of thirteen and sixteen) is about *the shell of self-centeredness.* As securing social independence from family becomes more of a preoccupation, the adoles-

cent now pushes against parents for more freedom to grow. Withdrawing into greater privacy at home, the young teenager pulls away into the preferred social company of peers with whom to explore and adventure in the larger world.

This is perhaps the most intense period of adolescent growth, as the boy or girl becomes extremely self-concerned. Now the teenager is increasingly focused on immediate gratification and is more likely to act inconsiderate of parents. In response, they often have to confront to get heard, interrogate to get important information, argue to get their household needs met, and do battle to get compliance with family rules.

More than at any other stage, conflict seems to rule their relationship. Parents must often oppose what the teenager urgently wants in order to protect his or her best interests. Now they are sometime adversaries instead of constant friends.

For those parents and the only child who have had a history of childhood harmony, they may have little practice managing the disagreement, frustration, and estrangement that they now feel more frequently. Because of this inexperience, parents are *vulnerable* to overreacting. They may say in anger what they have later cause to regret. Or they may *underreact* by letting go or giving in on issues that they later wish they had spoken up about and opposed.

3. *Late adolescence* (typically occurring between the ages of sixteen and eighteen) is about *the unreadiness for independence*. As the negativity of early adolescence and the conflict of mid-adolescence start subsiding, a new emotional energy—*anxiety*—begins to take their place.

Now the dream-like fantasy of independence that excited the twelve-year-old's imagination becomes a scary reality for the older teenager approaching the age of graduating high school. Instead, being embedded in a world where the time that mattered most was the present, the late adolescent is forced by growth and circumstance to consider the future. "What am I going to do with my life? If I'm going to move into an apartment with a friend, how am I going to pay for that? If I'm going to get a job, what job? If I'm going on for more education, where will I go to school?"

Most late adolescents don't have clear answers to these questions, and this ignorance, as well as the prospect of figuring out a next step, are frightening. "But I'm not ready for independence!" thinks the teenager, and parents anxiously agree. This anxiety that can create a *risk* for parents who are not inclined to let the son or daughter go until he or she is totally prepared for a successful launch.

Now, at this late stage, they may choose to become suddenly active in their child's life, trying to "fine-tune" the young man or woman by giving a crash course in the finer points of managing independence (servicing a car, balancing a checkbook, filing income tax). In the process, conflict is usually provoked by their well-meaning but ill-timed efforts. The older adolescent is not about to tolerate this interference: "I can figure out all that stuff on my own!" To make matters worse, when parents share their many worries about the child's unreadiness, they only reinforce worries of the child's own. Finally, in their anxiety, they can give many variations of a confusing double message: "We are ready to let you go, but we still intend to hold on."

4. *Trial independence* (typically occurring between the ages of eighteen and twenty-three) is about *the challenge of living on one's own.* During this final stage of adolescence, the young man or woman is experiencing true independent living for the first time and usually finds the footing extremely slippery. With so many more demands to deal with than anticipated, for awhile he or she cannot manage to meet them all, attending to one at the expense of others.

There are so many commitments to keep—rent, academic standing, bills, employment demands, legal requirements, credit obligations, personal promises, family engagements—that he or she usually breaks a few along the way. Surrounded by a cohort of other insufficiently prepared friends who are also learning independence the hard way, everyone seems to be stumbling and falling, getting in and out of difficulty. The young person's social world can be very unstable at this time, chaotic with change. To make matters worse, this is often the period of maximum drug and alcohol use and sexual acting out, so there are very real dangers to beware.

All this evidence of mistakes and misadventures sooner or later points to incompetence, only proving what both the only child and parents feared—that he or she is not fully capable of managing all aspects of adult independence. Now a significant dip in self-esteem can occur for the only child, making him or her extremely *vulnerable* to parental disapproval when self-doubt is so strong within. Compared with them, he or she feels so incompetent, whereas parents may be so stricken by concern about their child's trials, that they succumb to criticism to correct, punishment to control, and the expression of despair when neither intervention seems to work.

Even though the eight to ten years of their child's adolescent growth can feel confusing to parents, it is a lawful process. That is, certain developmental changes, tensions, conflicts, and problems tend to unfold in sequence as the teenager disintegrates the old boundaries of childhood to make way for growth to adulthood to occur. While he or she is growing up, parents are doing some growing of their own. They are gathering maturity, the key to which is maintaining sufficient perspective so they do not take the changes in their child personally. Adolescence is not something children do to parents. It is a process of growth they go through with parents. And there is a world of difference in being able to make that distinction.

To help parents help their only child navigate the uncertain passage through adolescence, the next four Keys will describe some supportive strategies they can employ during each of the four stages that have just been described.

38

~~~~~~

MODERATING RISKS FROM EARLY ADOLESCENCE

KEEPING A POSITIVE PERSPECTIVE

B ecause it is so easy for parents to become preoccupied with their only child's contrary behavior during *early adolescence*—the negative attitude (dissatisfaction and criticism), the rebellion (active and passive resistance), the beginning experimentation (testing limits to see what can be gotten away with)—it is important that parents find ways to maintain a positive connection with their son or daughter during what can be a trying time.

If they fixate on their difficulties with the child, they are in danger of getting into *reductionist thinking:*

- "Our child is *nothing but* a problem";
- "Our child *only does* things wrong";
- "Our child *never gets done* what we ask."

Locked into this simplistic frame of mind, parents can unwittingly harm their only child for whom, despite denial to the contrary ("I don't care what you think!"), parental faith and approval remains vitally important. At this time of separating from childhood and beginning to socially separate from them, the child needs support, not censure.

The challenge of parenting during early adolescence is to keep a positive perspective. To maintain this frame of mind requires understanding that any child is always more than the sum of his or her problems, which only constitute a very small part of a very large person.

A child is *not* a problem. A problem is just some aspect of their child to which parents take offense or wish to change, or about which they feel concerned. Lose sight of this reality, and the child may too: "My parents are right, I'm nothing but a problem!" Now all the strengths and resources necessary for recovery in their only child have slipped from view. The boy or girl may feel inclined to fulfill the partial vision that discouraged parents see: "I might as well give up and act as bad as they think I am!" When parents lose sight of the whole child, the likelihood is that the child will too.

Simply because the early adolescent offends some parental tolerances, challenges some parental rules, and tests some parental limits doesn't mean that the child should be treated like his or her relationship to them is broken. Parents must normalize the relationship after every disagreement and corrective encounter with a statement of affirmation so the child understands that he or she has not lost loving standing in their eyes.

For all these reasons, during early adolescence, it is important that parents communicate a number of encouraging messages to their only child when times get tough.

- No matter how "bad" the child acts, parents let it be known that they always see the larger "good."
- No matter how severe the child's problems, they always let it be known that they see the child's greater strengths.
- No matter what is going wrong, they always let it be known that they notice all that is going right.
- No matter what the child has still left undone, they always let it be known how they appreciate what else he or she has accomplished.

39

^^

MODERATING RISKS FROM MID-ADOLESCENCE

PROVIDING LOYAL OPPOSITION

Because it is so easy to become embroiled in conflict with their only child during *mid-adolescence*—when the push for social freedom becomes most intense and consequences of irresponsibility can cause so much harm—it is important that parents model the management of differences with their son or daughter in constructive ways. They need to beware the extremes of underreaction and overreaction.

Underreaction

Parents typically *underreact* to unacceptable behavior in order to avoid conflict and emotional discomfort. "We just hate fighting with our son. He gets so angry and unhappy. He resents our corrections, and then gets down on himself knowing we are down on him. We've about decided it's just not worth the fuss. It's easier to let most stuff go. After all, the most important thing is for all of us to remain friends."

During the only child's mid-adolescence, "being friends" with their son or daughter should *not* necessarily be the highest priority for parents. To maintain harmony in the relationship at the expense of teaching the child safety or responsibility is not a good trade-off. The mid-adolescent who is not socialized to work within the rules at home is ill-prepared to get along with other authorities—teachers at school, employers in the workplace, and agents of the law out in the world. Parents must be willing to put their popularity at risk during mid-adolescence in order to adequately socialize their child. If more conflict is the cost, then so be it. They must be willing to assert *the five pillars of social authority* in the child's life, taking stands the boy or girl may not like.

1. "We will *set limits* on your freedom where we feel the risks are too great or your responsibility is insufficient."
2. "We will *make demands* upon your time and energy to meet family needs."
3. "We will *ask questions* when we want to know about what is going on in your life."
4. "We will *confront issues* of concern with you that you may not want to discuss."
5. "We will *apply consequences* for serious misbehavior to encourage you back into obedience."

Each assertion of parental authority can be an invitation into conflict for the independence-minded child. It is also an opportunity, however, to let the mid-adolescent know that parents are committed to keeping a protective family structure around the boy or girl at this impetuous and impatient period of growth. They will not be backed away from this responsibility by the intensity of his or her objections.

Overreaction

Parents typically *overreact* to mid-adolescent conflict out of inexperience with serious argument with their only child. Unpracticed from not having conflict with older children, they feel unprepared for the adolescent boy or girl now challenging them to battle. Fearing loss of authority if they do not prevail, parents may feel justified in going to any lengths, even to hurtful ones, in order to reassert control. "We don't like it, we don't want it, and we won't have it. She's never treated us this way before, and we are not about to allow it now. We will do whatever we have to in order to show her who's in charge. She will learn to respect the stands we take, or else!"

Fighting to establish dominance at all costs is *not* a constructive way for parents to conduct conflict with their only child. When being right, when showing the child who's Boss, when winning, when not backing down, when having the last word are all that matter to parents, then they are at risk of behaving as if any means, no matter how damaging, justifies the end.

What helps moderate this risk for doing hurt is for parents to accept that their child has now left *the age of command* (when he or she believed obedience was largely unquestioned and automatic) and entered *the age of consent* (when he or she now believes that authority can be questioned and obedience is a matter of choice). Now parents must often work through some degree of resistance (delay, complaint, argument, initial refusal) to get the cooperation they want. Resistance is both an attempt at independence and at saving face. "Before you get your way with me, I'll try to get some of my way with you. If I don't, at least I'll get to have my say."

Another danger that parents face in overreacting is encouraging their only child to do the same. Because conflict creates resemblance, strong-arm tactics of one party tend to encourage the use of strong-arm tactics by the other. By modeling hurtful behavior in disagreement—yelling, insulting, name-calling, threatening, resorting to physical force, for example—parents set the standards that become the rules by which the adolescent learns to conduct family conflict in return.

Guidelines for Conflict

It helps if parents can remember some simple guidelines when contesting a difference with their only child.

1. Foremost, remember that the *process* of conducting the conflict is usually more important than the *outcome* reached. To win the battle of wills by wounding their only child damages them both. The child experiences betrayal and resentment; the parents experience remorse and guilt. (The damages are reversed if it is the child who inflicts the harm.)

2. They need to keep the conduct of conflict emotionally *safe*. Conflict must never be used as an excuse for doing injury to another family member. Conflict is only intended to work out inevitable human differences in their relationship, differences that tend to become more common and intense during their child's passage through mid-adolescence.

3. Should they or their child experience harm in the conduct of their conflict, then the differences at issue need to be set aside and the violation of safety fully discussed. The injured party needs to express the hurt, and the offending party needs to listen, and some agreement must be reached so that injury will not be committed again.

4. Each party is responsible for monitoring his or her emotional arousal. If frustration at opposition is about to cause anyone to do or say something damaging, then he or she has *the right of separation* (to declare a time-out, to walk away and cool down) as well as *a responsibility to return* after having regained rational control (to take up the unfinished issues and carry them through to resolution).

5. Finally, and this is particularly important for an adolescent only child, parents must absolutely maintain *loyalty* to their son or daughter in conflict. The boy or girl must feel assured of their underlying commitment: "No matter how hard you push against us, you cannot push away our love for you."

40

MODERATING RISKS
FROM LATE
ADOLESCENCE

KEEPING ANXIETY IN CHECK

B ecause it is so easy for parents to become worried
about their child's unreadiness for independence during *late adolescence*, it is important that they manage
this anxiety without undercutting the only child's courage
and resolve to leave. What can help parents at this point in
their parenting is to remember that almost no late adolescent
child departs from home fully experienced with the array of
responsibilities that accompany increased self-support.
Whether starting to share an apartment and hold a full-time
job, or starting to live in a dorm and go to college, there will
be a host of unfamiliar demands and problems for which the
young man or woman will be unprepared.

Perhaps 60 percent preparation for independence is
about as much as most parents can provide. That done, they
must turn their child over to the *Big R*, Reality, and *The School
of Hard Knocks* in which he or she must learn the rest.
Therefore, if parents insist on delaying the only child's departure until he or she is "all ready," they will never let their son
or daughter go. *Some degree of unreadiness for independence
is not a problem for the late adolescent. It is a fact of life.*

Fine-tuning—trying to cram last-minute learnings for independent living into the child's high school senior year—only provokes conflict and reinforces what the child already fears: "I don't yet know enough to make the next step on my own." As for parents directly expressing worry to the late adolescent about negative possibilities that might occur, these are usually received by the older teenager as a vote of no confidence when his or her own self-confidence is already feeling pretty low. Because their son or daughter has enough worries of his or her own, parents do better not to burden their child with any more, but to keep them between themselves. What the late adolescent needs is a strong statement of faith by parents that he or she has what it takes to learn from new experiences the necessary skills for independent living.

Double Messages

Most important, in their ambivalence about letting their son or daughter go, parents need to beware giving a series of double messages that can weaken the only child's resolve to break the final ties of dependence upon them.

- "We know it's time for you to leave, but we don't know if you can handle the responsibility" (thus, they sow the seed of *doubt*).
- "We want you to make your own decisions, but we think you are making bad choices" (thus, they sow the seed of *disapproval*).
- "You are free to go, but your leaving leaves us all alone" (thus they sow the seed of *guilt*).
- "You don't owe us anything, no matter how much we have sacrificed for you" (thus, they sow the seed of *obligation*).
- "We want you to have your own social world of friends, even though you are leaving us with no company except ourselves" (thus, they sow the seed of *pity*).

Instead of communicating these messages that put their only child in a very painful double bind (wanting to leave/not wanting to leave), parents better serve the late adolescent by using words that can free him or her instead.

Helpful Messages

- "We believe you have what it takes to learn from life experiences whatever else you need to know" (thus, they make a statement of *confidence*). Thinks the child: "They have faith in my capacity."
- "We believe in the importance of you making your own choices, whether we happen to agree with them or not" (thus, they make a statement of *respect*). Thinks the child: "I don't have to lead my life exactly their way."
- "As you leave for this next stage in your life, we are excited for you" (thus, they make a statement of *support*). Thinks the child: "They love me enough to let me go."
- "Just having had the pleasure of parenting you is all the return from you we could ever ask" (thus, they make a statement of *sufficiency*). Thinks the child: "They do not expect me to pay them back for all they have given."
- "Just as we want you to enjoy making a social world of your own when you leave, so we will continue to have a satisfying social life of our own when you are gone" (thus, they make a statement of *independence*). Thinks the child: "Even though I am their only child, I am not their only significant source of social company."

41

MODERATING RISKS FROM TRIAL INDEPENDENCE

EXTENDING PARENTING SUPPORT IF NEEDED

I t is easy for parents to become concerned about an only child who is unable, for the moment, to make or keep some of the major commitments required by *trial independence*. It is hard to help the young man or woman out and not injure their child's self-esteem or enable dependency instead.

What complicates this last phase of adolescence for parents of an only child is that *many only children tend to begin the adolescent process late*. There seems to be two reasons for this delay.

1. When life with parents feels so satisfying and congenial, the boy or girl may feel reluctant to modify a relationship that feels so good.
2. When bonding to parents is so tight and the importance of their approval is so great, the only child may feel reluctant to assert dissatisfaction with parents, push against their restraints, test their tolerances, challenge their authority, and pull away into the social company of friends, all of which are part of the entry into adolescence.

The effect of both factors is that some only children can begin adolescence as late as early high school. When this delayed entry is the case, a *collapsed adolescence* can occur, creating enormous pressure of change on both the teenager and parents over the next two to three years. The negativity of early adolescence is barely started before becoming compounded by the conflicts over freedom of mid-adolescence that are scarcely underway before the anxiety of late adolescence sets in. So much developmental change compacted into such a short period of time can create a high-intensity relationship for all concerned. It takes emotionally stable, clear-thinking, firmly resolved parents to help the adolescent safely navigate this stormy passage.

When a collapsed adolescence occurs, the only child's period of trial independence is frequently protracted. In this case, parents may have to extend their active role several years beyond what they might normally expect—even into their son or daughter's mid-twenties. Such an eventuality is perfectly okay because there is no official timetable for growing up that must be met.

What is not okay, however, is for parents to communicate to the young man or woman that he or she is letting parents down by not yet entirely letting them go, or rescuing the son or daughter from consequences that if faced could strengthen the child's capacity to learn some more adult responsibility. Sometimes the best and hardest help to give is the refusal to help. "No, we won't give you money to prevent the repossession of your car. How you cope with it is up to you."

Returning Home

Suppose, however, that the demands of independent living prove too much for the only child the first time out? Suppose the *freedom of choice* ("All my decisions are up to me"), the *personal responsibility* ("All my well-being depends on me"), and the *social distraction* ("All my friends are always having a good time") prove too much to handle. Perhaps, having flunked out of school, having lost a job, or having been overwhelmed by unpaid debts, the only child wants to come home for a stay, to depend upon parental support while gearing up to try independence once again.

The challenge for parents at this point is to welcome the child back ("We want you to know we are always here for you"), to expect accountability for decisions made ("We want you to take care of any unmet obligations you incurred away from home"), and to be clear that the stay is a time-limited one ("We expect you to use this temporary period back home to regroup your resources, to rethink your plans, and to prepare for your return to independent living").

Being Supportive

Mindful that trial independence for most young people is a mix of *slipping and sliding* (breaking some commitments) and *drifting without direction* (not yet being settled on a course in life), parents need to keep their responses constructive during what is a particularly vulnerable time for an only child. "Coming home to live with my parents at the age of twenty-six feels like such an admission of failure. The last thing I ever want to do in this world is to disappoint my parents by not living up to their expectations. But here I am, supposed to be doing well, and so far everything seems to be going wrong!"

At this critical juncture, parents need to be emotionally supportive.

- Affirm *faith*, not despair: "Mistakes don't mean you lack what it takes to find your independent footing."
- Express *patience*, not criticism: "You need to take the time to think through what has happened so you can use what you have learned to grow."

157

- Offer *consultation*, not taking control: "Should you ever want our input, it is there for the asking, but you are not obliged to follow what advice we give."

The role of parents during their only child's trial independence is to accept the difficulty, respect the challenge, and encourage the struggle of achieving independent self-support.

42

THE IMPACT OF DIVORCE

DIVIDED LOYALTIES

In the United States today, an only child, no matter how beloved, is not exempt from a harsh statistic: *about one half of all marriages with children end in divorce.* Because he or she is so tightly bonded to parents and is usually such an integral part of their marriage, parental divorce is particularly painful for an only child. Not only is the world of family broken apart, the only child feels additionally torn by opposing loyalties to parents who are in conflict with each other.

Unanswerable questions can torment the only child. Which parent is at fault? Which parent's version of what caused the divorce is true? Whose side should the child take? Is there something the child can do to reunify the parents? How can he or she equally divide time and attention given to each parent after divorce so neither feels that the child is playing favorites or is being unfair?

The Emotional Impact

For the preadolescent child (up to about age nine), there is usually grief at the loss, anxiety about the future, and a question that he or she finds frightening to ask: "If my parents can lose love for each other, can they also lose love for me?" For the early to mid-adolescent child (about ages nine to sixteen), who is already in a state of rebellion against adult unfairness, the divorce only increases a sense of grievance and justifies a more ruthless commitment to selfish ends: "If my parents can put my wants and needs aside for their happiness, then I can put their wants and needs aside for my happiness."

For the late adolescent child (about ages sixteen to eighteen), often just beginning to explore caring relationships of his or her own, the boy or girl must now confront a harsh reality: "Love is not forever." A corollary to this first cruel understanding is a second: "All commitment is conditional." In consequence, the older adolescent child of divorce may either delay or avoid commitment, keep caring casual and superficial, or, for safety's sake, seek social and emotional control in the relationship. Each choice is made to prevent getting hurt, with the child mindful of the final lesson that divorce can teach: "The people we come to love the most can injure us the worst."

Easing the Impact of Divorce

There are a number of actions that parents can take to help ease, but not eliminate, their only child's painful journey through their divorce.

- If possible, *jointly* announce the decision to divorce to the child to show that although ending their marital connection to each other, both parents remain committed to working together for the future welfare of the child.
- Explain the new living arrangements and set up a *predictable* schedule of communication and contact with each parent, establishing some *flexibility* that allows the child to talk to or see the absent parent when that child has spontaneous need.
- Allow the child to set up personal *rituals* to ease the transitions of departure and reentry from visitation, and establish

household *routines* that give the child a sense of order to help stabilize his or her passage through this painful change.

- Encourage the child to ask any questions about the divorce and the future, answering them as honestly as possible given the child's level of maturity to understand. Information helps reduce fear of the unknown.
- Where possible, give the child some sense of choice in designing separate living conditions with each parent in order to help the boy or girl reassert some sense of control in each of the new homes.
- Commit to listen to some emotional protest (expressions of fear, anger, suffering, and helplessness) from the child in response to the divorce.
- Be patient with any short-term regression that may occur as the boy or girl temporarily retreats into more childlike behavior for security (clinging or whining, for example).
- Be prepared for some short-term lowering of academic motivation and performance at school as a function of emotional interference in the child's capacity to concentrate and study. Supervise schoolwork, but be sensitive to how the divorce is drawing off a lot of the child's energy as he or she daily struggles to adjust to divided family life.
- Do not depend on the child for emotional support, but exercise adult responsibility to provide emotional support for the child. If possible, provide an outside helper—family friend, extended family member, or counselor—who assumes special status in the child's life for the first year or so after divorce to be a confidential companion with whom private thoughts and feelings can be safely shared.

43

TRAVELING BETWEEN
PARENTS

REDUCING TENSIONS AND
MANAGING VISITATION

W hat if parents of an only child cannot emotionally reconcile their grievances against each other after the divorce? The best answer to this hard question is to ask both parents a harder one: "Do you love to hate each other more than you love your child?"

The Costs of an Unreconciled Divorce

Parents who refuse to come to terms of emotional acceptance with their divorce and continue to support mutual animosity, are placing their mutual grievances over their concern for the emotional well-being of their son or daughter. In doing so, it might be helpful for them to count the costs of this decision for their only child.

- The boy or girl is condemned to becoming an emotional carrier of parental animosity back and forth across visitation.
- Agonizingly conflicted by divided loyalties and the pressure to take sides, the boy or girl is vulnerable to becoming depressed. In order not to further inflame the parents' embittered feelings toward each other, he or she may decide to contain the anger and turn it inward rather than express it to them.

- Come adolescence, the only child of an unreconciled divorce may strike back at those who have inflicted so much hurt from their unresolved resentments by using their division against them. Becoming ruthlessly manipulative, the teenager can exploit their animosity against each other by threatening or offering to take one side or the other in order to get his or her way: "If you don't give me what I want, I'll get it by living with someone who will show they love me more."

Adjustment Demands from Visitation

Divorce is a separation of a relationship back into its individual parts. The initial personality, preference, and lifestyle differences that proved divisive of the marriage tend to become more pronounced between the mother and father thereafter. *Divorce increases diversity between former partners.*

As a result, the only child, who was so closely identified with the union of both parents, now finds visitation a process of differentiating himself or herself. The boy or girl now lives on significantly different terms with each parent, often activating different dimensions of himself or herself, depending upon with whom he or she is staying. "Since Mom is a late night person and Dad is an early morning person, my schedule really changes depending on which home I'm in."

Spending time with either parent can be an emotionally mixed and conflicted experience, with the only child often missing the other parent and longing for the close old days when both were still together, when the family union was intact. Holidays, birthdays, and other traditional occasions can be particularly painful reminders of how the family has been lost. It is a mistake, however, for divorced parents to come together at these times for the sake of the child, because unrealistic reunion fantasies tend to be encouraged: "Maybe Mom and Dad will get back together after all."

163

Because attachment to each parent remains so strong, visitation requires significant psychological adjustments for the only child, and both parents need to respect this complexity. They need to give the child emotional space to let go of one setting for the other, respecting the child's need for some time alone when returning from the other parent's home before engaging with the demands of the resident parent.

Unless one parent has cause to believe that the child's emotional or physical well-being is being placed at risk in the other home, it is usually best to leave the child free to manage that relationship, and to decide how much to share about what went on. What generally does *not* help is:

- to interrogate the child about the visit,
- to criticize the other parent for what did or did not go on,
- to demand of the other parent that living conditions in that home be changed.

Divorce effectively disenfranchises each parent from having any right (except in situations where neglect, danger, or abuse occurs) to request that the other parent change his or her way of living. Each must come to respect the other's separate sphere of family influence.

This respect is perhaps hardest to extend to lifestyle differences that one parent endorses by his or her actions and the other morally disapproves—living with someone in an unmarried state when the child visits, for example. The offended parent is usually not empowered to take legal recourse in these situations; however, that parent can still express concerns to the ex-spouse, and give another perspective on the situation to the child. "You need to know that I don't agree with the living arrangement in your other home. I can't change it or keep you from it, but I do have the responsibility to tell you exactly why I think their living together when you visit is wrong. As your parents, we obviously disagree on this. To decide what you believe, you need to hear both sides."

QUESTIONS AND ANSWERS

When a divorced parent of an only child remarries, are there any special problems for the child that the couple should anticipate?

Yes. Typically, after divorce, the only child re-bonds to each parent to compensate for family security that has been lost. In the process, when the child's primary residence is with the mother, for example, the boy or girl may come to occupy a powerful, quasi-adult family role—"man of the house" to the mother if a son, or mother's "best friend" if a daughter.

The longer the only child lives alone with a single parent and the more wed to one of these roles the child becomes, the more reluctant he or she is to give it up when a stepparent arrives. To some degree, the stepparent is seen as an outsider usurping the role of major companion to the child's parent, and asserting unwelcome adult authority in the home.

It doesn't matter if, during their single parent's dating phase, the only child and prospective stepparent got on well. Once remarriage occurs and they all move in together, the only child will usually resist this family change to some degree. Holding on to his or her old relationship with the parent, the child will oppose the competitive and intrusive influence of the stepparent.

Expecting this resistance, the parent and stepparent:

- can be clear and firm that there is nothing that the child can do to make this family change go away;
- can be patient and not punish the child's resistance, allowing it to gradually wear down into acceptance over the course of the first year or so of remarried life;
- can create opportunities where the stepparent and child can spend time together alone to get to know each other;
- can create opportunities for all three to do special things together as a family that the only child and parent never had a chance to do before;
- and can create opportunities for the child to have time alone with the parent with the stepparent not around.

Does an only child do better in a public or a private school?

Compared to their public school enrollment, a disproportionate number of only children seem to attend private schools. This is not surprising because parents of only children are naturally protective, are highly invested in their child's preparation, and often want to exercise a sense of choice over his or her education. For many of these parents, private schools offer a promise of stricter classroom control and increased social safety, a more academic focus and enriched curriculum, a more homogeneous and orderly student body, and the power to expect and enforce expectations that students will pay attention, follow rules, and do their work.

Like any choice, however, this one is double-edged: for what may be gained, something may also be lost. Compared to attending public schools, private schools can be a sheltered and limiting experience, providing a less adequate social preparation for functioning in a larger, more impersonal, and more diverse world.

Public schools also generally offer more extracurricular activities in high school to all students, and more support services in general, than do their private counterparts. Academically, the high-level courses in public schools tend to be comparable (and in some cases superior) to what private schools provide.

One shortcoming of private schools is that parents, although paying customers, have less constituent standing and advocacy power in a private system than in a public one. If they don't like how the private school is serving or treating their child, the school is not obliged either to listen or to act on their concern. Parents may simply be told to take their child and leave. In a public system, however, parents are citizens of the community who have elected representatives on a school board to whom they can appeal if the local campus or central office refuses to give them a satisfactory response.

Public or private? Parents just have to weigh the needs of their only child against the costs and benefits that each kind of education has to offer.

Are there some children in multiple-child families who show many of the characteristics of being the only child?

The *first child,* of course, is in fact the only child for awhile, although parents with additional children in mind from the outset usually maintain the perspective that he or she is "only" for awhile, and is destined to become one of more. The first child, however, is often the lead carrier of parental expectations and has a lot of special standing to lose when dethroned by the arrival of the next in line.

Special needs children, however, because of their relative degree of physical, learning, or emotional disability, can absorb a disproportionate amount of parental energy, time, attention, and family resources. Compared to siblings, they are more developmentally challenged and therefore can require more care.

In the process of becoming the primary family focus, the special needs boy or girl can acquire some of the characteristics often associated with being the only child—used to being the center of parental attention, used to being treated with special consideration and care, used to being unusually closely attached to parents, to name a few. Parents tend to make an extremely high investment in this child to maximize growth and independence.

The challenge for parents is how to give the special care required without throwing the entire family system out of balance. They do not want to ignore everyone else's needs for the sake of one. Here are some possible guidelines parents might want to consider:

- If risks from being an only child become apparent in the child with special needs, where appropriate, moderate those risks in some of the ways described in this book.
- Resist the temptation for obsessively doing "everything possible" for the special needs child when that ambition creates significant neglect of the parents' own well-being, that of their marriage, or of the other children.
- Become well informed about the nature of the disability and helpful resources available, and locate like parents with whom to share parenting ideas and emotional support.
- Accept their own and other children's occasional ambivalence toward the needs of the special child. Do not punish their own ambivalence with guilt. Do not blame the other children for sometimes feeling resentful, jealous, shut out,

lonely, abandoned, or even socially embarrassed. Don't shut these feelings up; talk them out.

• Finally, value all the love that the special needs child has to give to and receive from family members.

Why is our only child breaking contact with us a few years after leaving home?

There comes a time, after *trial independence* is over (around age twenty-two or twenty-three), when many adult children enter a period of serious self-examination by asking themselves a very powerful question: "Why am I the way I am?"

At issue is confronting some of *the unfinished business of childhood* (growth yet to be accomplished) and *recovering from childhood wounds* (healing emotional injuries sustained while growing up), both of which may now stand in the way of effective adult functioning and the capacity to form satisfying intimate relationships.

In the process of looking back, the adult child identifies influences that had hurtful and helpful formative effect, among the most powerful of which are feelings of grievances about, and feelings of gratitude for, things that parents did and did not do. This historical inventory becomes partly an evaluation of parenting received. Because the best that parents can give any child is a mix of strength and frailty, good decisions and bad decisions, wisdom and stupidity, most parents get mixed reviews. *Often, before the adult child can claim the good side of this mix, he or she has to address and express the bad.*

For parents of an only child who have always been close, this period of evaluation, with its separation, lack of regular communication, and occasional expression of hard feelings through critical remarks, can feel extremely scary. Wonder the parents: "Will our only child ever want an ongoing and loving adult relationship with us?" In most cases, unless significant trauma was experienced, the answer is "yes." The adult child just needs time and space and to come to terms with the family past so he or she can go freely forward into a workable adult relationship with parents. Parents can help this process along in the following ways:

- by keeping faith in the relationship,
- by continuing to affirm the constancy of their love for the child,
- by holding themselves in readiness for the child when he or she is ready to reengage with them,
- by exercising patience and not, in panic, trying to take control,
- by communicating a willingness to noncritically listen to whatever the child would like to say,
- by being willing to answer any questions about the past that the child might want to ask,
- and by openly acknowledging that they were not perfect parents but simply gave a full-faith effort to do the best they could on his or her behalf.

How will the marriage of our only child alter his or her relationship to us?

"Children always mean more to parents than parents mean to children." (See Suggested Reading, page 175 [Sifford 1989, 170].)

The only child's marriage brings this observation home, and parents need to respect the primacy of this new commitment. Marriage does not mean that they are loved any less, only that their child has now found someone, a partner, to love more.

Having been number one in their only child's life for so long, this change can feel like a threat and a demotion. It does not have to be either, however, if parents:

- celebrate their child's capacity to make this adult commitment,
- commit their love to the new son- or daughter-in-law,
- and begin taking pleasure in the extended family that has now begun to grow.

How should we respond to pressures to have more than one child?

Recognize them for what they are: either *ambitions from other people* who will not have the responsibility for raising your additional child, or *insecurities within yourselves* worrying about whether having one child is adequate family enough. Yielding to either source of pressure is *not* a good basis for deciding to have another child.

- Parents do not owe each other, society, their parents, their friends, or their only child another child.
- Parents do not need to plague themselves with doubt about whether adding another child will improve the upbringing of both children. It will not.

Given sufficient time, parenting an only child provides parents the real-life experience necessary to honestly assess whether they want to emotionally, energetically, and financially afford to support the additional demands of another child. Both parents must be in agreement. If the vote is split, then the answer is at least "not yet," and perhaps "not ever."

Should we believe all the stereotypes we hear about only children?

Emphatically "no." Parents need to resist the negative pressure of social stereotypes that often seem to stigmatize the only child, and themselves, for deciding one child is enough.

The stereotype says the only child can be: selfish, solitary, insecure, spoiled, possessive, bossy, cautious, dependent, and peculiar. But in truth, the only child can be: generous, social, confident, considerate, sharing, collaborative, adventurous, independent, and normal.

Parents of an only child need to rest assured that a single one can be as happy and healthy as one of many.

GLOSSARY

Adolescence The period between when a young person leaves childhood, around the age of puberty, and finally grows up enough to undertake adult independence eight to ten years later.

Adultize To encourage a child early in life to precociously acquire adult skills, attitudes, and bearing.

Androgynous Having psychological characteristics drawn from both sexes.

Collapsed adolescence When a child developmentally delays entering adolescence until high school, causing early, mid-, and late adolescence stages to unfold in a very short and intense period of growth.

Compulsive overparenting When excessive worry drives parents to try to control their child's life, to eliminate all risks and to attain all of their goals for the boy or girl.

Crushing statements Critical comments parents can make that can cause their child to experience an extremely painful loss of standing in their eyes.

Deficiency beliefs Internalized beliefs about himself or herself that cause the child to feel inadequate or inferior no matter how hard he or she strives to prove otherwise.

Dream agendas When parents attach their own unfulfilled dreams to ambitions that they want their child to accomplish.

Emotional enmeshment When a parent's and a child's own emotional well-being depend on the emotional well-being of each other.

Emotional extortion A tactic of manipulation in which the intense expression of emotionality is used to overcome resistance from the other person in order to get one's way.

Fine-tuning When parents try to cram last-minute learnings for independence into the late adolescent before he or she gets ready to leave home, typically attempted during the senior year in high school.

Proactive parenting When parents act to develop in the child a capacity for responsibility that will be useful when the young person assumes independence at the end of adolescence.

Reductionist thinking When parents begin to think of their child in simplistic terms, as "nothing but" a particular set of traits.

Synergy of pleasing The dynamic in relationships in which efforts to please each other increases each other's desire to please.

Trial independence The last stage of adolescence (roughly between the ages of eighteen and twenty-three), when the young person is struggling for the first time to live on his or her own.

SUGGESTED READING

Mulford, Philippa Greene. *Keys to Successful Stepmothering*. Hauppauge, New York: Barron's Educational Series, Inc., 1996.

Newman, Jill. *Parenting an Only Child*. New York: Doubleday, 1990.

Pickhardt, Carl E. *Keys to Single Parenting*. Hauppauge, New York: Barron's Educational Series, Inc., 1996.

Pickhardt, Carl E. *Keys to Successful Stepfathering*. Hauppauge, New York: Barron's Educational Series, Inc., 1997.

Pickhardt, Carl E. *Parenting the Teenager*. P.O. Box 50022, Austin, Texas 78763, 1983.

Pitkeathley, Jill and Emerson, David. *Only Child*. London: Souvenir Press, 1994.

Sifford, Darrell. *The Only Child*. New York: Putnam's, 1989.

INDEX